The Late Interiors

Also by Marjorie Sandor

The Late Interiors

A Life Under Construction

Marjorie Sandor

ARCADE PUBLISHING

Arcade Publishing books may be purchased in bulk at special discounts for sales promotion, corporate gifts, fund-raising, or educational purposes. Special editions can also be created to specifications. For details, contact the Special Sales Department, Arcade Publishing, 307 West 36th Street, 11th Floor, New York, NY 10018 or info@skyhorsepublishing.com.

Arcade Publishing® is a registered trademark of Skyhorse Publishing, Inc.®, a Delaware corporation.

Visit our website at www.arcadepub.com.

10 9 8 7 6 5 4 3 2 1

Library of Congress Cataloging-in-Publication Data

Sandor, Marjorie.
 The late interiors : a life under construction / Marjorie Sandor.
    p. cm.
 ISBN 978-1-61145-005-7
 1. Sandor, Marjorie. 2. Authors, American--20th century--Biography. I. Title.
 PS3569.A5195Z465 2011
 813'.54--dc22
 [B]
                          2010052665

Printed in the United States of America

Grateful acknowledgment is made to Naomi Shihab Nye and BOA Editions for permission to reprint "My Friend's Divorce," from *Fuel*, and to University of Pittsburgh Press for permission to reprint lines from Larry Levis's poem, "The Perfection of Solitude: A Sequence," from *The Selected Levis*.

These essays originally appeared, in some cases in slightly different versions, in the following publications:

"Greenhouse Dreams," *TriQuarterly*; "Visitation," *Prairie Schooner*; early sections of "A Gardener's Journal," *Chattahoochee Review*; "Fall Planting" (under the title, "Threshold"), *Fugue*; "On Our Streets" (under the title "Junior"), *Prairie Schooner*; "The White Cat," *The Fairy Tale Review*, subsequently reprinted in *My Mother She Killed Me, My Father He Ate Me: Forty Contemporary Fairy Tales*; "Orfeo's Oyster," *Peanut Butter, Gooseberries, and Latkes*; "Word Music," *Opera News*; "Butterfly on the Blackboard," *Oregon Humanities Magazine*; "Capistrano Days," *Ninth Letter*.

Dedicated to the memory

of

Ann Cline

1942–2001

CONTENTS

If my mind could gain a firm footing, I would not make essays, I would make decisions.

—Montaigne

Then I took the top off the softened gold nib of one of my fountain pens, the one that runs best, and I did not write. I let the night, the long night, minister to me. Nights, like bodies, stretch themselves as the fever of summer leaves them.

—Colette

Prologue:
Greenhouse Dreams

But would not working among green things make for a certain bliss?
Harmony, peacefulness? What had disturbed the Nurseryman that
he was drunken among his growing things? . . . If you, among
healing flowers and leaf, got a kind of madness, what about us lost in
the bloomless? If the green be mad, then what of the dry?
                                        —William Goyen, "In the Icebound Hothouse"

The greenhouses of the state university are clustered on Orchard Street, on the western verge of campus, and of town. One winter night I happened to walk past them with a friend, a male colleague from my department. What harm in it? Two people in winter coats, bundled up against the cold and dark. But we found ourselves curious: How was it we'd never noticed these greenhouses before?

We paused, leaned forward over a hedge, cupped our palms to the glass. There were vines staked in pots, some wilted and strangely crisped, others lushly gleaming. Our breath fogged the view; our palms left smudges on the window. We sprang back, and as we walked away, we turned our coat collars up, peered around corners, behaved like spies.

But in the joke was a faint, brief leaning, a bumping of shoulders in heavy coats, and, just as quickly, a pulling away. It was nothing. We were good friends; we taught together. Besides, I was married and had a young daughter. His wife had recently left him, but she sometimes drove up to the front of his house and parked there until he came out.

These greenhouses are long and narrow, with gray concrete foundations, set about with the high green armor of privet hedges. All that winter, they—and we—were gazed down upon by orange streetlamps. Deep in the winter night the glass buildings whispered a fertile, incubatory gossip, the murmuring talk of the after-hours, the unmarked hours, under their own orange lamplight. Picture the brick walls in alleys behind city nightclubs, for this is the light of greenhouse seduction. We walked past them a second time, and a third. We yearned to get inside, to be touched by what surely must be a rare and silken air, unknown orchestrations conducted on an ordinary street, unmarked, unsupervised. Surely there we would be stirred into dreams by a faint breeze coming from a source we couldn't see, seduced into putting one finger tenderly to the pale green lifting, lifting, from the precise dark soil of birth. How could one not go mad, just wanting to get in?

We didn't break in. We were law-abiding citizens. It was enough for us to lean over the hedges, put our palms up to the windows, and peer in, like novice cat burglars or peasants at the prince's window, sussing out the scene of the crime—for at night, the greenhouses looked vulnerable, unobserved by the Authorities, like jewel cases in a museum, the day guards gone home to bed and no night watchman in sight, just the two of us, left alone with the jewels in glass within glass. Surely alarms would sound if we dreamed seriously of Trespass.

And besides, what would become of us if we went further? It was enough to have secret dreams, to pray to be lost, like those children who walk through doors into kingdoms unsuspected, into a time not measured in this world, for in a greenhouse, time is not measured in seconds, let alone minutes—how dull, how enormous and heavy an interval we live in! A plant breath was the measure we wanted to know, the slipping breath of frond and leaf and infant bloom, opening, opening, all night long. Daytime they grew, too, of course, but we didn't care. It was the night that interested us; night, when the plants and their growing belonged to us.

Did we pause too long at the windows one night? For now we began to notice the number of locked doors and forbidding signs. "AUTHORIZED PERSONNEL ONLY. DANGER, KEEP OUT" we chanted, suddenly insouciant. We leaned forward, wiped the windows clear of fog, saw, and *almost* knew. Asked each other innocent questions: Are those potato vines? Tomato plants without tomatoes? Is it all right that I'm in love with you?

Above one long table a light snapped out, all by itself. The others continued to blaze.

By spring we'd sinned—cupped faces in hands, and kissed. How different they looked to us now, those greenhouses, stern holders of the keys to righteousness, where, by day, orderly researchers worked with steady logic, wisdom in their smallest moves, never lurching or leaping, untoward, past a necessary step. They understood that it was safer, smarter, *better for everyone*, to knit the earth together by measuring the harvest between days, the white fields between words. One must not ask for more. We'd been like that ourselves, only months before. Law-abiding all our lives, good children, careful and obedient, afraid to distress our parents. Oh, to simply walk past those greenhouses now. To be able to say, We're still just friends, aren't we? We're just stirred by the possibilities of breaking and entering, though it would not be to steal, we said to ourselves, but only to breathe there, to say, just once, I have penetrated the greenhouse, I have been inside.

And then, like good citizens, to go back to our regular lives.

Oh, to be a night watchman, a guardian of greenhouses in sleep: that must be restful, a calming occupation. Then desire would be tamed. But maybe not, with all that glass, all that watching, the sound of a thousand plants breathing, making their terrible secret plans. Possible diseases, taking root at the cellular level even as you watched, seeing nothing, not a flutter, not a breeze. (Though what were those great fans outside, what engines did they run?) And— a new thought—what of insects? It wouldn't be possible to keep them out. No doubt the researchers infested the plants on purpose, just to see what would happen. What terrible experiments might a night watchman witness? Or would the quiet murmur of growth and decay be enough to drive him mad?

It was midsummer when I confessed to my husband. The little halting words spread through all the small roots of our small town, from hallway to hallway, house to house. By August, when my colleague and I walked, we passed the greenhouses in daylight, without stopping, without turning our heads. On we walked, past the university barns for sheep and pigs and cattle, out to where the creek rushed swollen under the white bridge, beyond, beyond, like children with a destination deep in the wilderness, their parents fast asleep at home. Should we turn around? We didn't know how, or when. So we just kept walking.

By autumn, I had moved out of my house, into an apartment on the other side of town, where my daughter, now seven, joined me half the time. A strange calm descended, a blue calm of wood smoke and rotting leaves, of everyone busy again with the dramas of their own lives. And gradually, slowly, we ventured out on our walks again, sometimes taking Hannah with us. One night, we discovered two greenhouses we'd not noticed before—not on the edge of campus this time, but deeper in, between Theatre and Philosophy. They were old, these greenhouses, and had a frosted delicacy the others did not, like Russian hunting lodges in fairy tales, cupolaed and spired, the old windows deliciously milky. Hannah, coasting past on her first bicycle, looked long and hard at the Philosophy building and asked, "Why are there pictures of plants on their tiles?"

A good eye, a discerning eye. Once upon a time, we told her, they studied plants in this building, too. We didn't say what else we were thinking: may she have, along with that discerning eye, a forgiving heart, a gift for adaptation.

It is winter again, the season of greenhouse dreams. Two years have passed, and still they tendril their way north and east, calling us out from the house we have found together, milky white itself, with dark green shutters, across from Chemistry and behind the university's student Catholic center. "'Where were the greenhouses going . . .'" my lover says. "It's a poem by Roethke, I have to find it." He searches among his books until he finds his Roethke, finds the poem; it is taped now to our refrigerator, along with Hannah's yellow Post-it note: *Sorry, we're not home, we got eaten by tarantulas.*

Our home isn't far from the great humming engines of the greenhouses, engines of danger and disgrace, the shock of touching the secret, dangly roots of love. Sometimes late at night, we think we hear a secret singing. And not long ago I noticed, beneath the western windows of our kitchen, a greenhouse beginning. When, and by whose hand, did this come to be? Was it really mine? It must be, for look, here stands an old wooden table crowded with plants. In the late afternoon, sunlight collects there.

We are gazing at the corner together, my lover and I, talking about greenhouses. "Did you know," he says, "that they actually draw in the light—by their very design?" And he makes a fantastic, incantatory gesture, both hands up, then drawn to the body, as if pulling in the last of the light to hold it close, capturing it for the coming dark.

Summer
2000

Property

We bought the house, Tracy and I, because we "fell in love with it." I put this in quotes to acknowledge our naïveté, but the truth is, I'm not feeling the least bit detached. It's a love affair with a dwelling place, and irony still gets down on its knees before knock-down, drag-out love. We turned the key in the lock, opened the door, and there it was: a beauty we recognized, and didn't.

The perception of beauty, like anything else, must surely be a dynamic thing, a pulse and counter pulse. On the one hand, we might be trying to recapture something about childhood: a long-lost comfort, an early moment of safety. And on the other, we are pulled forward by the possibilities, even the dangers, of what we don't yet know about the beloved. So there is hope and trepidation: a contrapuntal composition all its own. A symphony of memory and longing has been set in motion, apparently for a house, an inanimate thing, a piece of property that we are privileged to be able to afford in the first place.

Is that really what it is? Yes, and no.

Recently, at school, Hannah learned the word *property* in science hour, as in "the properties of soda": its characteristics, or attributes. After school that day, we went to a coffee shop for a cookie. She looked around with pleasure, pointing at the wooden counters, the ochre- and pumpkin-colored walls, the low lighting, and said, "I like the texture of this place. I like its *property*." Is it possible that her first associations with the word might not have to do with ownership, but with the quest to define a substance?

Surely part of our pleasure in buying this house was a sense that we were stepping into a small quixotic adventure of our own. This is no doubt a bourgeois notion, the absurd trembling of two middle-class university professors for whom buying an old house is *an adventure*. But it is, for now, our world. Our friends and family declared themselves "charmed" and "enchanted" but ultimately dubious about the wisdom of our decision to plant ourselves on the very doorstep of the local university. Soon, they said, "the bloom will be off the rose" and we'll find ourselves besieged by that unstable tribe known in university towns as the "student element."

But there's another way to think about it. The architectural critic Grant Hildebrand says that along with a sense of refuge, the human seeker of a dwelling place is also looking for—even craving—peril. Would Hildebrand accept my borrowing of his theory to suggest that this house, an island in a sea of young people newly sprung from their own childhoods, might have enticed us with its potential for peril?

I'm joking, and I'm not. I suspect we hungered for our own little narrative of quixotic rescue—the desire to create a hermitage in a human wilderness. Is this the double longing that sang in our bones as we crossed the threshold for the first time? For the place had the hushed quality of a sanctuary—an island of peace in the midst of a constantly changing population, a mixed-use neighborhood itself in constant flux. Maybe that's what we were after: to experience the tension, the boundary itself, between an interior texture, the very *property* of safety and intimacy, against the natural grit and excitement of change.

The house is nearly a hundred years old, built in 1915, a mix, we've been told, of Craftsman and Colonial. Its first owner was a professor of horticulture specializing in tomatoes, an Englishman aptly named William Bouquet, who had one of the first gardening radio programs in the West. Since his era, only one other family has lived in the house. By the time we stepped inside, it had been carpeted, wallpapered, linoleumed, Pergoed, repaneled in the upstairs bedrooms, and otherwise layered over by decades of domestic "improvements," and it felt dark and cloistered. Yet through all its trials, its bones, its essential character, had remained intact. The second owners, the Wilsons, had left the original woodwork of the staircase, living room, and dining room untouched. There was a glass-fronted bookcase in the living room and a built-in china hutch in the dining room, and across from the dining room's windows, old fir paneling of an intense reddish brown, shining and spotted in places as if generations of children had leaned against it, sighing. There was no getting around the house's power to enchant; even those things we'd spent a lifetime smugly rejecting now seemed to call out to us: grandmotherly lace curtains, a half dozen oval portraits of the Virgin Mary guarding various rooms, a small wooden shrine in the back, painted the same green as the house trim, and containing a foot-tall Virgin.

Neither of us said it, but the house was our Sleeping Beauty, and we, together, her prince, pushing through the brambles to throw open the doors and curtains, and awaken her with a kiss.

So a narrative of rescue was planted, as it sometimes is in love: we would rescue this particular beauty, one who'd slept nearly a hundred years, waiting for us. That's part of falling in love, isn't it? Suddenly you are capable of a singular tenderness. You want to tend to the beloved, with all her imperfections, vulnerabilities, this sacred body that others have rushed past, briefly admiring, but too smart about flaws and future troubles to slow down and really see. Can you fall in love with a house the way you would with a person, the way I did, at least, when I was an adolescent? Always I was drawn to the slightly pale boy, the lousy athlete with a gift for the jazz trumpet or a passion for the distant planets. Something trembled in him; something not yet bloomed.

And then there's the added pleasure of falling in love with a place with someone you've fallen in love with. To look at it, and to touch it, with four hands instead of two. Now not only Sleeping Beauty comes to mind, but also that mysterious novella by Alain-Fournier, *Le Grande Meaulnes*. In that book, two French schoolboys, on an afternoon walk, discover an old estate; inside, a girl sits at a piano, wearing a mask. At the end of a magical timeless day, they must leave, go back to the school. But the estate, this lost domain—

and everything that happens within its brambles—becomes a sacred space they'll spend their whole lives trying to find again.

We made an offer. Don and Mary Wilson, the older couple who had raised nine children in this house, were at first wary of us. Devout Catholics, they had done some "checking around" in our small town, and had discovered that we were not married. But our real estate agent was confident. "Don't worry," she said. "They want to sell." Why so desperate, we wondered, and were told that it had partly to do with their advancing age: the stairs were too much, the house too big now, without the children. Later that summer we would begin to suspect that they knew the larger changes planned for the neighborhood. Knew, and did not say.

Our friends remained skeptical. They bade us open our eyes and look around: at the three-story apartment complex across from the house and, only one door away, Monroe Street, the university's motley, ever-changing thoroughfare, composed of cafés, pubs, and shops. Did we grasp how noisy it might be? Yes, we said. At the time, the local establishments ranged from the candlelit and golden-walled Magenta to the fluorescent East Ocean Buffet, built inside a former copy store. Between them lay a sandwich shop and a former tuberculosis hospital that had morphed, in the last few years, from bookstore to tanning salon to tattoo parlor. Among the protean businesses farther down the street, one holdout from the distant past remained: a tiny, ramshackle tailoring shop where three old women sat chain-smoking before their sewing machines, surrounded by great tilting stacks of fabric.

Yet the house felt protected from the activity. To our immediate north lived our block's only other family, the Dearings, in a yellow Victorian. And to the south and west, shielding us from the university itself, was the Newman Center, a gathering place and chapel for the university's Catholic students and faculty.

We were ready to embrace it all: the pedestrian stream on our street, the tattoo parlors and sandwich shops, the exhausted graduate students in their dark coats stumbling out of Chemistry, and the night cries of the young issuing from their pubs, possibly to mate. A whole miniature urban world, like something in a snow globe. Each of us had lived, in our twenties, in big cities—Tracy in Houston, myself in San Francisco and Boston—and we both still craved the movement, the excitement, of those years and places. It's a hard parallel to make convincing, here in this college town we jokingly call "Bucolaland" or "Cow Valley," but the truth is, we relished the sight of students walking to Chemistry, to the library, to classes. At ten minutes to the hour, they made a steady stream past the house's front windows, tousled, sleepy, lost in their own dreams. There were two rather dull flower beds out front, packed with mats of lithodora and something in a sad, variegated gray, and I imagined replacing these with more vibrant, less tidy plants, for students and teachers to take in as they passed. What color might best float across a girl's memory during her History class? A dark blue delphinium, for instance. What childhood memory, faintly hooked to what sleepy desire, might be triggered by the afterimage of dark spiky blooms? Maybe her mother used to take her, in her stroller, past neighborhood gardens. And might this memory attach itself, nodelike, to a strand of emotion and make her lift her head a certain way, drawing the attention of the boy in the next seat over, moving the drama of her life this way instead of that? There was no telling.

We quickly came to appreciate the Newman Center for the protective sense of enclosure and retreat created by its five brown-shingled Craftsman cottages, its courtyard with a towering elm and fir. In the following months, we would learn that the houses had been designed, and the trees planted, by a late-nineteenth-century medical doctor, Margaret Snell, who, in 1889, was appointed professor of household economy and hygiene here, and established the first college of home economics in the West. She was lovingly nicknamed "the apostle of fresh air" for her belief that loose-fitting clothes, a cold morning bath, and an open window in all seasons could restore health and happiness to young women. Not only had she planted those courtyard trees, but, we'd later learn, many of those in the town's Central Park and in its downtown.

All this seems marvelous enough in retrospect. But it would be a few months before we felt the urgency to learn the history of those buildings and trees. In those early, heady days of moving in together, we took for granted the shelter they offered, a shimmering, wood-and-green buffer between the house and the big institution just a few steps away.

Those cottages also told us where we were. They spoke in the vernacular of the Pacific Northwest, a place that still felt exotic to both of us. The biggest one, named "Hillside" by Dr. Snell herself, had a gable roof and mullioned windows with flared hoods that jutted out, fairy-tale-like, on the corners. On rainy days in particular, it looked as close to *tree* as *house* can get.

And there were the trees themselves. What a shock we got, during our first visit to the house, as we walked through to the back and emerged onto a cedar deck, to see behind our yard a magnificent canopy of trees, with the elm and fir at its center. It seemed miraculous—we laughed, using the word—but seriously, how could it be, so close to campus and downtown, that so many great trees had been planted, cultivated, saved. It looked, back there, like there was no city nearby. Just a moving canopy of various greens, a canopy changing with the seasons—the elm waved its branches in the downstairs bedroom's skylight, over the place where our bed would go.

Sanctuary. It felt like that, in those early summer weeks of establishing a home, long before we knew that we would need a place for Tracy to heal after open heart surgery; long before we heard the first rumors that the whole Newman Center complex of Craftsman cottages, and most of the trees, were threatened with demolition, to be replaced by a block-long, four-story student-apartment-and-commercial complex called "Newman Commons." By autumn we'd see the plans for a monolith of brick and glass, designed to "pick up" the look of the institutional buildings on the university side of Monroe Street, and to "echo" the "residential, single-family" dwellings of its immediate neighbors on Twenty-first Street.

Twenty-first Street. That would be ourselves and the Dearings.

That fall, it would be hard for us to see how a four-story building the length of a city block, containing sixty-four student apartments and a tall glass lobby featuring a central clock tower and a cross, might "connect" or create a transition to the single-family dwellings on the west side of Twenty-first Street. The language was smoothly persuasive. The sort of language we all use to brush past trouble, to bring change, or to tamp it down.

One night at dinner, an architect friend tried to help us understand. This is a man who loves old houses and their histories but who has also learned, by serving on our town's planning commission, to be pragmatic. At our table he closed his eyes, looking for all the world like Marlow, in Conrad's *Heart of Darkness*, gazing into the Thames as the tide goes out, black barred clouds hanging ominously over the horizon.

"It's amazing, how hard it is for people to accept change," he said.

I couldn't—or was afraid to—read the expression on his face. I knew he was trying to tell us not to be unrealistic fools; not to imagine that we could preserve the small urban sanctuary we'd stumbled into.

A moment later he shook his head, softened his voice. "Though, I admit," he said, "if it were happening in my backyard, I'd be kicking and screaming too."

Kicking and screaming. I thought of the complete phrase— "dragged away kicking and screaming"—and shivered a little. He hadn't said it, but now I heard it: the hint of a breeze of an implication that this had been coming for a long time, from long before we bought the house. I remembered the real estate agent saying, "Don't worry, they want to sell."

But all this was still to come, as was our fight to save the old buildings and trees. It was still the height of summer, and we were still impetuous lovers, pushing aside the brambles, opening the creaky rusted gates of the lost domain. Our armor was nothing more than a barber's tin plate and a broken lance, but we didn't know it yet. For not-knowing, too, is a property of the newly in love: to ignore, with the singular genius of a naïf, little rumors of reality, of inevitable change.

Visitation

for my daughter

One February morning, not long after I left your father, my own father came to visit me. He'd been dead over twenty years by then, and you were barely six. Do you remember, before we moved into this house, the apartment we occupied for a while, with its linens and forks and pans all furnished, the woodstove we used every night in fall and winter? Rooms that felt like sanctuary but never quite home, that held the strange delights of the temporary bivouac but also the underbelly of fear, for it was the place to which you came every other week without promise or choice, under your parents' agreement of joint custody. It spooked me, I can tell you, now that you're a little older. Under my feeling of temporary safety lay a darker note I never let rise up: a feeling of deep insecurity that maybe underlies all our dwelling places, maybe underlies our passion for "decorating" once we convince ourselves that we own a space, and can somehow control what happens in it.

How appropriate that my father should visit here. A ghost in a ghostly, in-between place.

A short hallway connected your bedroom with mine. It was covered in dark brown linoleum, icy cold on your toes when you got up for school those winter mornings.

That's where I saw him: my father, the grandfather you never met. He was standing in that hallway between your room and mine; those two identical rooms with their pale yellow walls.

15

It was early morning, and you were still asleep. The night before had been one of the difficult ones. Tears and bathwater and pajamas. I held you close on the landlady's pale blue nubbly sofa. It makes sense now: for what else would bring the dead back like that, with such urgency, indecipherable messages fluttering in their hands? For there he stood, at dawn, in the icy hallway, and I could see that he was struggling to make a decision. Should he look in on you, the grandchild he'd never known in life? But it seemed he needed, just as desperately, to tell me something concerning himself, his own well-being. It was clear from the way he gripped the doorknob that he was in a terrible rush.

"I'm glad you're here," I began. "Hannah—"

"Listen, sweetheart, no time to talk," he replied in his old gruff way. "I need you at the hospital. I'm dying all over again."

"Oh, Dad, I can't," I said. "My little girl's sleeping—"

"Hurry," he said. "Please—I don't want to bother your mother. She's been through enough."

"But I can't," I cried.

"Are you sure?" he said, and he gave me a look I can neither forget nor properly describe. Not a look of disappointment, or of accusation, or even of self-pity. He knew how his story would go, that was all. He knew everything, and still could not resign himself to the way it had gone, the way it had to go.

"Well," he said with a sigh. "You can't blame me for trying. Good-bye."

Surely there was more, but here, my memory fails. The blue twilight of winter dawn and you, my little girl, what woke you? For here you came, skittering across the linoleum of the hallway, its true emptiness, its terrible distance at last revealed now that he'd gone. You stood by the bed a moment, then got in under the covers, wriggled and pushed me over, loving and aggressive all at once. Flannel pajamas, cold toes, soft hair, the fragile blue of your eyelids. Oh, what will happen in your life?

I closed my eyes and invited—no—*willed* my father back, but he did not come. When at last I got up to make our breakfast, the unfinished feeling was as powerful as an undertow; the icy linoleum, the pale blue carpet, all were emptier than they'd been before.

An absence, once announced, cannot be taken back.

Gardener's Journal

I'm starting this garden late. Late in the year, late in life. I'm so anxious to green everything up, to look out the back kitchen windows and see a wild and fully aged profusion—as if I have already lived here with T and Hannah for ten years or more—that I am in danger of criminal haste. On the other hand, what if I simply plant, semi-helterskelter but with a gambler's passion, then revise as I go?

Nine children were raised in this house. Does this have something to do with its depth, its deep green atmosphere? How else to put it? "Lived in" doesn't quite say it. It has gravity, rootedness, a kind of sighing, old, good slipper feeling to it. Dark varnished wood and small-paned glass bookshelves. We've pulled up the Wilsons' beige Berber carpet and revealed the honey-colored oak floors beneath, and propped T's big Bruegel print of *The Harvesters* against the fireplace mantel, all pale yellows and greens, peasants in various stages of exhaustion and effort, under trees, in fields. The painting goes with the house; that, too, seems a nice mystery. Anyway, the house feels voiced to me, choral and breathing and serious, deep in its bones: here we will make a sanctuary, and maybe I'll grow the sturdier character I feel down at the bottom of me, still not awakened but there, there.

Where was I?

The house? Nine children! All are grown now, but bits of mail still come for them, so many names.

And then there's the garden. It's like a story framed but unfilled, waiting for whatever hand will shape it. Don Wilson, a retired agricultural economics faculty member, told me that it was only this winter that he and his wife put in the raised beds. Raised beds—sounds delicious; but these are set off in geometric shapes by ugly orange-colored logs deeply staked into the ground. Kris, our friend the painter, says in her marvelous, definitive way, "Get a crowbar and yank them out of there." But I can't wait to see life there, so in the meantime I have planted one bed and half of another. Began digging before I'd finished unpacking. T has gone to teach fiction writing for ten days at Warren Wilson College, in North Carolina, so I'm indulging my sense of private bachelorette messiness, leaving bags of manure here, discarded pots there. Will I always?

The soil, when I began to work it, was dry and wretched-looking, and seven inches down, I hit the newspapers: three or four layers of them, damp but intact pages of the *Corvallis Gazette-Times*, still quite legible. Layer upon layer. I dug up some of it, but not all; somewhere along the line I just plain wore out. But where I *knew* I wanted to put something deep, like a Pacific Giant delphinium, or a Don Juan climbing rose, I dug with violence.

I have neglected to say that I have been swerving, hypnotized, into nursery parking lots and the local farmers' market, filling the back deck with homeless plants, *then* buying planting compost, and bag upon bag of chicken and steer manure. Hopelessly backward. But once I had the soil moistened and enriched, I began to put in the first batch of plants.

So, in the raised bed closest to the back porch, and near the north-side fence we share with the Dearings, are the following plants, their colors and heights only vaguely considered: Eight dahlia bulbs—apricot yellow, hot dark pink, another yellow, very spiky. So far, only one green stalk has emerged. Oh, where are you all, how long will it take? Did I plant you too late? Also two lavenders, three delphiniums, one red Maltese Cross, one lemon-yellow yarrow, and a bright gold coreopsis. And behind all of those, already clinging to the chain-link fence, a deep purple *Clematis jackmanii*. I want to cover the whole fence with climbers of one sort or another. More roses, another clematis. Oh, and honeysuckle, which my friend Martha, a graphic designer, says will "clothe the fence in no time flat." The other day when she was here, she waved her hand just once and I saw the future: a leafy wall splashed with little white trumpets of scent.

In the next row forward will go the following: tomatoes, peppers, okra, garlic, chives, arugula, and Red Sails lettuce, purely for its name. Closer to the gate, but still in the bed, some little yellow blooming thing and a purple groundcover.

Cart-before-the-horse is my flawed modus operandi, but look how it motivates! I must get them all into the ground before they die.

Wallpaper

Hannah has announced that she wants her room *different*. At nine, she's already got a defined sense of style and, I'm pleased to say, more confidence than her mother. As we discuss the possibilities, it emerges that she wanted either my study, which is small and square and an unholy mess (I'm flattered that she finds it cozy), or, failing that, an exact replica of her room at our old house—now her father's.

I am humbled by her desire; I want to do something. Maybe a square room *does* confer more safety, more containment, than a rectangle. I keep thinking she'll love the wonderful western windows of her long room, with their view of our own dogwood and blue spruce, and the Newman Center's elm, fir, and aspen beyond that. But she clearly doesn't care about the trees. I must face the true nature of her need, expressed in a matter of geometry. Could she be trying to stitch together her two disparate bedrooms, the two halves of her split life: the one at her father's house, six blocks away, and the one here?

She might be trying to restore her own sense of sanctuary, to piece back together the vessel I broke trying to make a new one for myself.

Sometimes, as a child, I woke in the dark, not knowing where I was. In those moments, all the known compass points of my bedroom meant nothing; the end of the bed, the bookshelf, the door frame, all of it was new and unknown. It took me forever to recognize them again, and for the interval, I might as well have lost my name, my sense of family, of belonging.

Now I need to imagine that fear in a young person who is literally moving, week in, week out, between two spaces—trying to keep her own compass steady, make the two feel like one. When I try to imagine this, the old terror rises, a gulf of black. But I have to keep trying. A little at a time.

The next morning we make a compromise. We rearrange the furniture until we've created two squares: a "bedroom" square and a little study square. It's quite cozy now. She lies back on her bed in its new corner, arms folded under her head in a relaxed and satisfied pose, for a whole minute; then up she leaps and starts composing, on the window shelf beside the bed, the one thousand and one artifacts of her young life: shells, marbles, tiny horses, the colored-sand-in-a-bottle from last summer's Renaissance Faire, the gel pens and Silly Putty and a china swan from the dollar store—this from the person who likes to inform me that my purse is full of unnecessary things!

But even as I say this, I'm aware that only half her stuff is at our house, and that as she collects and rearranges these talismans, she must be feeling the absence of those things that live at her father's. It seems deeply reasonable, even necessary, this need to keep everything within view, a stay against abandonment.

Over the next few days we move, imperceptibly, from revising the "shape" of the room to choosing floor and wall colors. The walls she wants to be like those of my study, a pale yellow with white trim; the splattered red-painted wood floor, creamy white. We shake hands on the deal, and ten minutes later she's gone, in that breathtaking way of hers, off with her dad for a week in Sun Valley for a family reunion.

Once she's gone, I pull everything out of the room and start peeling off the little edge of pastel wallpaper around the top of the walls. Mostly it refuses to come all in a piece, and I leave tissue-thin bits hanging out of sheer indolence and irk. But in one spot, it comes off with a vengeance and, with it, a layer of painted paper beneath.

Suddenly I'm in another room, another era. This world is a sweet, faded green: sage-and-pine-colored tendrils tipped with delicate white flowers. Sage and pine. A memory floods in, of childhood summer afternoons in the San Gabriel Mountains northeast of Los Angeles. Through the color, I smell a place: sage and chaparral, the vanilla scent of the Jeffrey pine. The dry earth and, once in a while, the sharp, intense odor of the arroyos, the dry riverbeds, after a hard rain. A smell that makes me almost dizzy with longing.

There's a name for this scent: *geosmin,* literally, earth smell. The human nose is, for whatever reason, particularly sensitive to it. Geosmin turns out to be more verb than noun, more process than product; it's made by microbes and released when they die. An odd cycle to consider: a death creating an odor that in turn inspires a memory. A strange form of renewal.

Toward the end of the day I discover another layer of paper that doesn't want to let go. This one is handsome, too: a tan background striped with honey-colored stalks of bamboo. The peeling process reminds me of the erratic experience of writing. It reveals, in some places, this pure ancient green, and in the others, stubborn monuments of honeyed bamboo, fragments of paper shaped like nations. I chip at these boundaries to see more green, but even as I strive for more continuity, and to uncover further that shade of green that awakens memory in me, I'm drawn to the tension they create between them, the counterpoint. In the end, I decide to leave one whole wall and the area around the door frame unpainted, the two ancient papers speaking to each other on the wall. I'm about to stop when I chip one spot a little too hard and find, beneath both papers, a burst of a yet deeper honey—a rich Italian plastered look—and a delicate stem of red cherries.

It's hard to say no to this third—and surely deepest—layer. But I must. I leave a little medallion of it in one corner, like a signature, wash my hands, and call my mother. I want to share the discovery with someone, and the memory, too: of childhood, of the San Gabriel Mountains. She listens patiently, then gives a little laugh.

"I have no idea how to picture this," she says. "But I believe you. The big question is, will Hannah like it?"

How can she *not* like it, I want to say. All those delicious surprises exposed, with their questions and possible stories: who chose the green, and why; who wanted bamboo, and when? My only fear is that once she has glimpsed the little cherry sprig on Tuscan honey, there will be no rest until we have exposed it all.

We'll cross that bridge when we come to it, I tell my mother.

It reminds me, she says, of that word, what is it? *Pentimento.*

After I say good-bye, I have to look it up.

Pentimento: reappearance of earlier underlying painting when layer added later becomes transparent, revealing artist's change of mind, etc.

The word derives, it turns out, from the Italian for "repentance."

Weather

It's not just the wallpaper that's in layers here. The weather in the Willamette Valley itself seems to emerge from under other weathers, alternating, emerging, and disappearing. It is a peculiarity of this place that while there are still the last red leaves on the maples in fall, the azalea buds are already beginning to open in anticipation of spring. And meanwhile, it's raining, off and on, off and on. The rain itself is of a special variety. In Scotland it has its own name: *drow*, which signifies not only a cold, wet mist but also a bout of illness and a malignant spirit. Suffice it to say that the drow in Oregon is so light that you feel like an idiot if you get out your umbrella, but nevertheless, it soaks you through. Old-timers call it "the dry rain."

If we're lucky, we'll have what they call a "sunbreak" as we move toward spring or, better yet, a streak of hail. On such occasions, even the soberest of us will feel the wild pleasure of schoolchildren whose routine has been disrupted. That's how starved we are for weather drama.

There are other forms of confusion. In May, there comes a warm spell of such authority that everyone rushes out to buy tomato plants. Then the rains return, and the chilly nights, and for a week, maybe two, the tomatoes sit tragically, turning silver at their tips. By then the dahlias have gotten the green light, and up they come. Then the rains return, and the dahlias' tender shoots are chewed down to their naked beginnings by starved slugs, those secretive harbingers of true spring.

It always gives me a little shock, the indecision of the seasons here, their tango of two steps forward, one step back, but so does the violence of the human reaction to it. You hear chiefly complaints, even outrage, as if people are talking about a crime done to them in childhood, or the desire for liberation from some original double bind.

The problem, of course, is that we have expectations in the first place. This itself is historical—not our fault. Former Southern Californians who now live in Oregon like to boast that where they grew up, there were no seasons at all, only temperate beauty all the time. This isn't really true. The fact is, many of them are the descendents of Midwesterners, and therefore only extreme conditions speak to their innermost souls: tornadoes, blizzards, summer heat spells so well-defined that people speak of them "breaking" when they're over, as if they were fevers. By these standards, okay, granted, Southern California has no seasons.

A university town is particularly full of bewildered and petulant transplants: besides the proud Californians and brave, bored Midwesterners, we have harried former East Coasters, and Southerners still carrying around an ancestral memory of Spanish moss and fireflies and slow summer evenings. And worlds of travelers from farther nations—who knows what dreams, what homesickness for lost weathers they carry.

For isn't that what complaining about the weather really is: a song of homesickness? Longing attacks through the weather. Why is this? The longing for the old, bad, but *absolute* weather of memory, not the insubstantial drow of the present moment. Whatever it was that we were used to in our old life, *before here*, is the flag of our lost nation, the standard we raise up in the foreign land, nomads of the long-lost weather of home, the last little piece of our claimable identity.

"Where I grew up," Tracy likes to say, "you could *smell* the rain coming."

And there's a family story about my own father, a Chicago boy stationed in Texas during World War II. My mother and he were expecting their first child and living in army housing in San Antonio. The story goes that he put my mother, eight months along, into the car, and drove south and east almost three hundred miles to Galveston, where a hurricane was predicted.

My mother still concludes this story with dark satisfaction: "A policeman had to turn him back."

My own favorite weather memory comes from my time in graduate school in Iowa. One winter night, in the midst of a fierce cold snap, my boyfriend and I went to a party, during which the temperature dropped yet again. It was, they said, *ninety below with the windchill*, and when, at the evening's end, we tried to start his car, nothing happened. Even the wheels seemed firmly attached to the pavement. We called the one taxi service listed in the yellow pages, and the man who answered said, quite cheerfully, "It's hectic, but I'll try to swing by." When he arrived, he simply honked, and when we opened the taxi door, we nearly collapsed. For inside was another hemisphere entirely: it was balmy, maybe eighty-five, ninety degrees, and calypso music was playing on the radio, loud. The cabbie himself was a big man, comfortable in a short-sleeved tropical shirt. The drive couldn't have taken long—my apartment was less than a mile away—but I remember it as much longer, like a Disneyland jungle cruise in the middle of winter, all parrots and alligators and low green branches hanging down, the fierce, extravagant pleasure of weather denial.

Clay

I ventured out to tackle the front garden of our new house today, the two little curved terraces that the Wilsons had planted in Blue Star lithodora, some gray variegated stuff, and four, maybe five clumps of calla lilies. I had other ideas, as people freshly moved into new homes do, but I also knew that first, a grim, necessary penance, a soul-searching act of soil revision awaited me. What I suspected was true: under the desiccated mats of lithodora lay a few inches of mulch and, below that, long endless sheets of black plastic and, under that, stark naked reality: clay. Clay soil, more accurately, that had had plenty of time to snuggle down and get good and compressed. And when I lifted the black plastic, there it was, smooth and self-satisfied, like freshly poured concrete. But I was prepared for this, and began to dig—which, in the case of clay, gives new meaning to the word.

Lift, heave, chop. But sing, too, for the soil of this valley is legend. It is, in truth, mostly silt, with a varying percentage of clay in it, depending on where you are in the hundred-mile stretch between Portland and Eugene, bounded on the west by the Coast Range and on the east by the Cascades. The bottom line is that it's *silt* that makes the valley's soil so fertile: silt deposited here during the great Ice Age floods of glacial Lake Missoula. So we gardeners cannot complain. Nor can we justifiably kvetch about clay, as it has its own garden virtues: it retains moisture well, not to mention necessary nutrients like potassium, magnesium, and calcium.

It has other virtues, too, some of which could seduce you away from gardening altogether, and into more arcane obsessions. Last year, at our town's summer festival, I saw a man with a moistened chunk of dark red clay in his hands, cradling it so lovingly that it gave me a little shock—he looked like someone considering an illicit affair. I was momentarily confused: did he know the secret to gardening with clay? And where had he gotten it?

"No, no, it's not for gardening," he said, with a faraway look in his eye. "It's not from around here, either." It turned out that he was part of a local group reviving the ancient art of building cob cottages and earth ovens, for which this stuff—Coast Range clay, abundant in the mountains that begin just a few miles west of our town—is perfectly suited. For the festival he'd made a wattle fence of flexible willow branches. Near this fence was a big plastic bucket, from which you could grab a handful of moistened clay mixed with twigs— a substance to make you dream of Devonshire cottages—and sculpt it into faces between the braids of the fence. These faces tended to come out looking primitive and spooky: cavernous-cheeked faces, werewolves, bat faces, and huge scary hands; yet what I remember best is how good *this* clay felt in my hands.

But I must turn away from temptation and humble myself before my own clay, and my own small plot. A mere twenty percent of my garden soil though it is, this clay still has the power to turn that soil both diabolical and familiar, like a job in real life. It demands patience, cool, a lowering of expectations. Every day I hack at it with my shovel edge to break it into smaller pieces, then kneel and work it in my gloved hands to get it down to smaller particles yet, my fingers as sore as they are after practicing a Mozart sonata for too long, or grading too many essay exams in a row—exactly that feeling. It comes out—the clay, I mean—in big hunks, precisely the smooth look of chocolate ice cream when the girl behind the counter takes up her scoop and plunges her powerful arm into the case and begins to work it, work it, to bring you up a scoop.

I have gained new admiration for the stamina of those girls. I promise never to romanticize their work again.

As it happens, one of my brothers is a soil scientist at Iowa State University. I badly want to call him up and ask him to tell me more about clay. We've already talked about it once on the telephone, and I know him: he'll say, with great patience, "What's your question?", for he is a man of science and doesn't waste language or wax melodic. But what I really want is for him to commiserate, to say, "Yeah, I know, isn't it the most damnable stuff to work with? Don't you just want to take a pickax to its neck?" I want to know if he's got pet names for different kinds of soils, if he's had loving feelings toward some and vicious hostility toward others.

I'll have to wait till he comes out for a visit, and when he does, I'm sure all these absurd notions will fall away. For, in fact, he's already corroborated what I've heard around here: that what we have in our yard is in fact fantastic stuff. Apparently, for gardeners, it doesn't get much better than this.

I must try to be content, even proud. I have tried to make the soil perform the little gymnastic acts he says it should: to form it into little ribbons and balls to find out its properties. But it's like trying to play classical music on the guitar when all you know are three chords and a primitive strum. It's not in my fingers. That's okay. Knowing the soil is "as good as it gets" settles me down; my brother has performed the function of a marriage counselor—for a woman and her soil.

Today I have a new question, one that I feel ashamed to ask, and certainly I will not ask it of a scientist. I want to know why this stubborn substance inspires such melodrama inside me. Why does it take me back to the primitive, wild reaction I had in childhood toward certain keys on the family piano? Their tones were personalities to me, and I struggled with them in imaginary battles. B-flat was a little villain in yellow tails; A, a fluttery maiden in distress. I conducted pianistic embroilments and affairs and huge wars and felt, briefly, a kind of satisfying, surging madness barely held in check.

But it was intimacy too, the real deal. I know that now, and what worries me is that I am beginning to feel this same passionate love-hate for clay. There is only one cure for this madness, and that is to go out and be with it. Curse the stuff if you must, but keep digging. Heave, chop, lift. Stay with it. Become a master of the form.

Gardener's Journal

The garden is in disarray. I can't attend to it properly, and while there's a good reason for this, I still feel negligent, guilty.

A few days after he came back from North Carolina, T began to have a squeezing sensation in his chest. It was a Saturday. He was moving a few more boxes from his old apartment to our house and had to sit down on the sidewalk. He thought it must be his asthma kicking in, though it felt a little different. He promised to call the doctor Monday morning. Then, Sunday night, at ten-thirty, we were making love, and he said, very simply, "I have to stop." His face was dark gray, the color of a new sidewalk or children's school clay. His eyes, usually blue-green-gray, had lost all color—I know of no other way to describe it. He sat quite still, clutching a pillow to his chest, but he didn't want me to call for an ambulance. When he was able, he got dressed and I drove him to the hospital. On the way there, at the intersection of Kings and Circle boulevards, amid houses and supermarkets and gas stations, a deer was crossing the street with fantastic dignity. I slowed down as carefully as I could, afraid to jar T, but it was he who called out, in the midst of severe nausea and pressure in his chest, "Watch out, there's another one." Sure enough, there was another deer, right in front of us, and I hit the brakes fast. I was afraid this would do T in.

What followed, in the next two days, is still a bit of a blur, though made simpler by the weird coincidence of Hannah being on a special "granddaughter only" visit to my family in Southern California. So I could concentrate fully on being at the hospital. It began Monday evening with a cardiac catheterization (T was their last patient of seven in one day: the nurse called him, quite cheerfully, "our add-on"). Within twenty minutes the doctor had come out, and said that T had 85 percent blockage in the left main artery and blockage in a smaller diagonal as well, and pronounced that he would have bypass surgery first thing in the morning. It's a mystery, this heart disease. T is in his mid-forties; there is no family history, he doesn't smoke, has very moderate, even spartan, eating and drinking habits. This is a Texan who doesn't really like the taste of red meat. In other words, nothing to forewarn. The cardiologist, a funny, fast-talking doc from Kansas City, put his hand on my shoulder, looked at me seriously, and said that our lovemaking had literally saved his life. If he hadn't had that sharp a warning, he would have been teaching his classes next fall and keeled over. They wouldn't have been able to save him.

I can only keep that sentence in my head for a few moments, but I want to try. That day in particular, I stood looking into the garden and held it in my head, at last knowing—but is there really any way to know?—how different this landscape, the whole world, would look with another version of those few words, with the story that so easily might have been. Secret stories wait inside each of us. The cardiologist says that these things don't happen overnight. The disease probably began sometime in his twenties.

Tuesday morning, very early, T had double-bypass surgery. At the nurse's station I was handed a beeper and told that someone would call me when he was "on bypass" as they call it; that is, once his heart and lungs were being kept going by a machine, and they could begin the procedure itself. Only later would we begin to grasp what that meant. A colleague visited T not long after and said, "So, during the operation, you were technically dead, right?" T looked at him in pure bafflement. Later, though, this remark drove him to look up CABG surgery on the Web, where he discovered that his heart had been cooled to 28 degrees, kept on ice—like an oyster—till the operation was over. In retrospect, I'm glad that I so naively went off with my beeper, not knowing what it means to be *on bypass*.

You have a few hours, the nurse said to me. You can leave the hospital with the beeper—it's probably a good idea to get out for a bit. What did I do? I remember clutching the beeper in my hand, not liking the way it felt hanging off the waistband of my skirt, so heavy on the summer cotton. I came home. Here. This place in which we had, so far, spent only a few weeks together. Standing in the front hall, I thought back to my blithe comment about indulging the messy bachelorette side of me. The house was still, silent, its depths cool and solemn and enclosing, offering exactly what we loved about it, from the moment we'd first stepped inside: the French doors between the dining room and living room, the tall windows and gleaming dark wood, even the Wilsons' old lace curtains, which Martha, with an unerring eye, had immediately said, "must go." She was probably right, but something in us wanted to keep them, to keep the old solid feeling, the sweet grandmotherly fussiness against the stately dark wood and stone of the fireplace.

I held off going into the garden. I had the terrible suspicion it had dried up in the eternity since Sunday night. I'd lost track of the weather. Had it been hot and sunny or overcast? Kris, with her wonderful surging energy even in the midst of her recent chemotherapy for lung cancer, had offered to water the plants. No, I'd said, I think it will do me good to come back and water.

At last I went outside. It seemed both momentous and absurd to water with the beeper hanging off my waistband. I was finished in no time at all; the garden seemed a bit detached, neutral in mood, somebody else's garden I'd been sent to water or, dare I say it, a neglected writing project. You come back to it after some unconscionable hiatus, and it gives you a tilted, cool look. A lover who will have to be courted all over again, from scratch.

It wasn't long after I got back to the hospital that the beeper sounded: he was on bypass, and doing fine. And within three hours, another call. He has "come through," said the nurse, and is in ICU. Don't be shocked when you see him. Lots of tubes, tape, and bruises. So I made myself ready, and when they let me in, along with our friend Ehud, there he was, bruised and zippered with scars, but sunlight was shining through the tall windows in the pale pink spacious room with all its machines humming and blinking.

The light is what I remember, the way it filtered into the room through huge trees on a summer day. If he could have turned his head he'd have seen them, but he was stuffed with tubes, in the mouth, the nose, postsurgery blood and fluids being drained out of his chest through an ugly yellow tube, and so only the helpless bystander could see that light flooding into the room. It flooded him, too, played on him quietly, so as not to disturb. The nurse sat at a little portable table, glancing up at him now and then, adjusting some dial or other. She was always there; it seemed such a gift that she was always there. Even the bubbling of the little pleurovac, the suction machine attached to the tubes, sounded oddly comforting, a little like the small stone fountain at home, the one he bought one winter day before we were together—pure indulgence, he told me once, a lovely phrase coming from his mouth.

Pleurovac. Sounds like the fall of tears in French. Or rain.

Yesterday I made a second trip into the garden. He was out of ICU and in a private room, a room already brimming with flowers and cards, and Ehud was with him, so I came back to the garden, this time dimly aware that the weather had been beautiful, warm but breezy, for three days now. And the garden looked different: no longer neutral and distant, as it had the day before, but tender, vulnerable, in need of a certain delicate attention. There would be no rough trampling between the okra plants to get to the clematis, whose delicate tendrils had fallen, unremarked, to the ground, and needed to be carefully lifted to the fence, to reattach. I saw, too, the depressions in the blue star creeper where I'd stepped, over and over, like a giant.

A little stone path might be a good idea.

The garden has become a place I no longer know. A place to which I will need yet another polite introduction, and a new, more tender approach.

July 20

T came home today from the hospital, and we've created a little sanctuary within a sanctuary: he is ensconced in bed, propped up with pillows, listening to Carlos Nakai's flute music and surrounded by books. No pain meds, thank you very much! He went off them the minute he was out of intensive care; they gave him terrible nausea. So to say that he's "resting comfortably" isn't quite accurate, but he is, certainly, deeply glad to be home. He declares he'd rather have pain than nausea any day. The nurses suggested "visualization" as a way of managing the pain without drugs, and the first time he tried it, a very specific memory came back: a beach in Belize where, as a graduate student, he once spent a blissful afternoon in a hammock, "lightly sweating" as he took sips from a bottle of cheap Mexican beer, "also lightly sweating," he recalls. Humid heat and shade are the elements in which he is happiest: in an earlier life, I suspect, he was a tropical plant.

After things slowed down, I called Hannah and explained T's surgery to her over the telephone in the least dramatic terms possible. She kept asking, "Did he have a heart attack?" and I could hear the alarm in her voice. "Not exactly, no," I said, for this was the truth. "He got lucky," I said. "He had a squeezing in his chest; that was the warning." Trying to put the experience into quiet terms gave me an unexpected moment of calm: Is this another form of "visualization"? A framing of something that was, in reality, sheer chaos?

Meant to say: while T was in the hospital, I stayed up late reading Grant Hildebrand's *Origins of Architectural Pleasure,* a calming occupation in its own right. One of the book's blurbs, by an architect named Juhani Pallasmaa, says, "In order to provide satisfactory domiciles for the urban dweller of the third millennium, architecture must continue to acknowledge the hunter, gatherer, and farmer concealed in the genetic coding of human behavior."

I like this: no matter how modern we think we are, these old selves still live in us, and must be acknowledged.

Hildebrand writes about the two needs of the hunter, gatherer, and farmer still in us. *Refuge*: a place of concealment, shelter, a place that in some sense speaks to us of safety. Think caves, groves, hollows. And *prospect*: enticement, peril, a place in which to hunt and gather. Wide-open spaces like oceans and meadows, with, as Hildebrand puts it, "open views over long distances . . . brightly lit, both to present a clear image of the landscape and to cast information-laden shadows—our fondness for sunlight may derive from its usefulness for this purpose."

All this has got me thinking about the first house I grew up in, the one in San Marino, northeast of Los Angeles, where we lived till I was fourteen and we moved to the beach. My parents had it built in the late fifties, after I was born and we outgrew the little house in Alhambra where they'd raised my three brothers. My mother's taste, from the get-go, tilted toward the spare and clean. She loved the work of Frank Lloyd Wright and, as she still puts it, "all things Japanese," and so the house had low eaves, cool terrazzo floors, and most of its windows faced a long narrow backyard planted with hardy Bermuda grass and camellia bushes. I never gave the house credit for its mystery and depth: as a young adolescent I labeled it *suburban*, and dismissed it for its lack of possibility. But now it seems full of mystery, and seems, also, to contain these very poles Hildebrand suggests we crave, biologically as well as aesthetically: prospect and refuge, danger and sanctuary. For although the house was slightly set back from the road, that road was a broad, busy boulevard with an island in the middle, a strip of Bermuda grass upon which my brothers and I played constricted but passionate games of Red Rover and touch football. The backyard, on the other hand, was sheltered by our own bushes and fence, and by our back neighbors' enormous live oaks and eucalypti. It was a veritable forest; we couldn't see their house at all. Was this a version of the threshold between wilderness and safety?

And inside? My mother kept it dark and cool in summer, shades drawn. Touches of warmth gleamed in that dark: copper vents over the living-room fireplace and the kitchen stove, a pale gold carpet in the hall and living room. Was she—unconsciously or otherwise—invoking the ancient comforts of cave and firelight?

I asked my mother once whether she and my father had worked with an architect and followed the theories of Frank Lloyd Wright or Japanese home design, but she only laughed and shook her head. "We just did what we liked, a little at a time, with a contractor," she said. "No architect, no overall scheme." Then she smiled. "My God, you couldn't get away with that now!" But I like to think that without quite knowing it, she was working out an ancient nesting-place desire: on the one hand, a need for interior peace and quiet, and on the other, a craving for adventure lingering from her own sheltered childhood in Indiana. Her mother emigrated to America as a young girl, her family forced out of Eastern Europe during the late-nineteenth-century pogroms. My maternal grandmother was a fiercely protective woman, right down to the way she kept house, always cool and dark and curtained. Was *she* unconsciously shielding her family from an ancestral sense of threat still echoing in her blood and bones?

Shades of refuge and peril might also exist inside houses themselves. I enacted, in that house, constant stagings of threat and escape, especially in the long, dark hallway between my parents' room and mine. This was a passage through which I played at "hunting" and "hide-and-seek" with my three big brothers, often feeling, on an ordinary afternoon, as though I were sneaking up on someone, or trying to move stealthily through enemy territory. The hallway frightened me sometimes at night, when I was feverish or distraught, or when, in the uncanny way of children, I suspected that all was not right with my parents. All this said, I passionately loved my small square bedroom, and until we moved to the beach when I was fourteen, I instinctively knew it for what it was: a refuge, my sanctuary. I didn't have the words then. But its corner position calmed me, as did the great California live oak in the Clarks' yard, into which I could gaze, lying flat on my back in bed and looking through the window to my left. I could stare at that tree for hours, its leaves like tiny green claws against the dark blue sky.

That was also my voyeuristic window onto the dangerous world, for through it, I could faintly see two of the Clark boys moving gracefully about in their shared bedroom, preparing for bed. And from it, at the age of seven, I made complicated plans with my best friend, George Miles, to go to a local park at twilight and help the Army of the Mice do battle to the death against the Army of the Rats. Out of that window I'd lean, late one evening, to say to George, *I don't think they're real. I don't think we should go,* only to be greeted by the disappointed set of his mouth, his dark, bewildered eyes. When he was gone, I sank gratefully into bed, heart pounding as if some enormous danger had been averted. But also dimly aware that my imagination had faltered at the test, and his had not.

July 25

T's been home from the hospital almost a week now. He's sleeping better, and the pain is decreasing day by day, though his back is quite sore—this, the nurses told us, is to be expected. We're thinking of hiring a massage therapist to pay a house call, just once. I want to use the phrase "out of the woods" but don't dare. But he's walking a little, too, farther every day: soon we will conquer the path to the covered bridge and the university cow barns.

Meanwhile, today I picked the first really ripe Sun Gold cherry tomatoes. There are fat bumblebees and small white moths everywhere, like something out of García Márquez's *One Hundred Years of Solitude.* The Don Juan rose is thriving, each bud a little fist of red petals that smell faintly of lemons, and are so dark that their edges go almost black as they unfurl. Just in front of the Don Juan, the sky blue delphinium has bloomed again, more sturdily and upright than its first time, and nothing looks remotely vulnerable, not as it did while T was in the hospital, though for the life of me, as I look back, I have not a single detail to offer you.

July 26

Things that have gone wrong in the garden: a list.

1. The bigger tomatoes. They look marvelous from above, but the first to ripen have rotten undersides, quite awful. In a few other cases, the plants themselves have grown very big and leafy but have hardly any fruit. Problem No. 1 is said to come from overwatering (this from Kris). Problem No. 2, I'm going to take a guess and say it was my novitiate's ignorance and haste: I fed the tomatoes in their pots plant food with every watering for ten days, till I reread the label and saw *once* every seven to ten days. Oops. Excessive feeding makes greenery, not fruit, Martha tells me. Sounds like life.

2. Black aphids have eaten and destroyed the gorgeous red nasturtiums in their planters; where was I? I'd better check Don Juan. There are ladybugs, fabled enemy of aphids, hanging out in the same goddamned planter, resting lazily on the lobelia and basil. How come they didn't knock out the aphids like they're supposed to? Too few of them? Or too many aphids?

3. In the bed where the old owners kept their statue of the Virgin Mary (they took the statue but left the grotto itself, a little green-painted wooden shelter—hereafter to be referred to as the Virgin Bed) everything's alive but the soft green moss (like Corsican mint, only not—what's it called?), which was perhaps too drought-sensitive for this spot, which gets a good six hours of sun a day. What other ground covers, soft but hardy, might go there? Creeping thyme? But do also note that a dark blue phlox I put back there hasn't done anything. Is this bed slightly doomed? What might be different about it? Let's watch and see, next year. There is the blue phlox on the left side of the shrine, and on the right side, two bee balms, one pink, one purple. We'll see what happens to them, I guess.

We've gotten ourselves a kitten, ten weeks old, a very sociable, easygoing female Manx with reddish-black fur, white paws and hind legs and chest. She was abandoned, and somewhere along the way, someone named her Katia. T has a special voice for her, and a special slurring accent and bunchings of words, bouquets of sound. Hannah, at nine, is very maternal with her, when she's not trying to get her to play harder or sleep in a certain position. Our friend Rich, Kris's husband, looked at the cat with nostalgia: "Ah, we once had a Manx. She was a lovely cat." Someone once told him this, which I liked: "If you're going to get a Manx, you might as well get a dog."

But I say, better a doglike cat than a catlike dog.

Someone did an I Ching reading for me earlier this summer, before T's operation. The answer came back: *Make only small moves, no great ambition.* Centering, conforming. I am supposed to use my intuition to make a safe place where like-minded people can be together.

Making love post-surgery seems delicate, dangerous, extraordinary.

Is it possible to maintain your privacy and be very expressive, intimate without exposing? I like M.F.K. Fisher's poise in the face of a wrenching sea change and grief. She left her first husband for another man, with whom she had brief but great happiness before his death from a rare disease of the blood, and all the while, she raised her two daughters. I admire the way she circles her darkest material, nearer and nearer, but always leaving the shocked heart silent. Also reading Penelope Fitzgerald, *The Blue Flower* and *The Bookshop*: both wry and comic in tone but drop-dead serious, absolutely harshly realistic about small-town small-mindedness, particularly *The Bookshop*, whose bleak ending shocked me in the best way. Also beginning to dip into Elizabeth David's *An Omelette and a Glass of Wine*. The introduction says that she is a purist about simple foods, an aesthete who is more and more shoved to the back of the bookcase. This, apparently, is what happens to purists over time. Such a fate only makes me more interested.

August 1

On staring at the garden.

Could do this for hours, checking for another stem of ripe Sun Gold tomatoes, a new bud opening on the Don Juan, one more tendril of blue star creeper reaching out to establish itself. The smallest sign of progress pleases me, and I think it's because another picture lies just behind my eyes: T inside the house as I stand outside in the garden. These days he is walking up and down the staircase for exercise, venturing briefly into his study upstairs, just for an hour at a time, to sift through books and papers, reacquainting himself with them as I do these tomatoes, these roses.

So, the garden: though I feel as if I could look at it, think about it, for hours, the actual transformation seems intolerably slow. I can't seem to *do* anything for a great stretch, but only in little dribs and drabs. Same way with writing, cooking, learning a little Bach piece on the piano. I do things in small spates (is *spate* a word, really?) then must float off to something else. Little bursts, then long stewings, then the urge gradually rises again, with its own swerving course of action. This doesn't seem a very efficient way to work, but it may be mine. Only if I live to be ninety will I get something done.

I was consoled to discover, recently, that the painter Pierre Bonnard worked like this. He kept a daybook in which he made very quick sketches and watercolors, with just a phrase like *vermilion in the orange shadows, on a cold, fine day*. He didn't paint *en plein air* like so many of his contemporaries, but took his daybook sketches, with their private language of hatch marks and circles and diagonals, which apparently stood for certain colors, back to his studio, and worked from memory. For him, it was all about memory.

One last phrase from his daybook: *Consciousness, the shock of feeling and memory.*

The painter Georges Roualt apparently invented a term, *bonnarding,* to describe his friend's method of "jabbing" bits of color on an unstretched canvas tacked up on the studio wall, working from memory, returning to the canvas repeatedly over a long period of time.

Thus it surely follows that to *prebonnard* is to stare through the kitchen window into the back garden, the eye coming to rest first on two green window boxes, one full of lobelia, sky blue with white centers, and some pure white; the other planted with lemon verbena and three kinds of basil, Purple Ruffles, African Blue, and Siam Queen. Oh, and nasturtiums, bordello-velvet red, which T's parents, visiting from Texas last week, politely plucked out of their salads and left on their plates.

"They're red," said his mother, laughing. "Isn't that the color of poisonous things?"

August 2

More plans, always more plans:

Out front on Twenty-first Street, rip out the black plastic in the two terraces. Break up the soil and amend. Plant bulbs and perennials, especially irises. Also lavenders and coreopsis. Keep thinking *drought-resistant* and *long-blooming*. Seems very hot and dry out there, not like the back garden at all. As far as annuals go, try cosmos, lots of 'em, and cornflowers.

Plant irises in front and back. Siberian, besides the ones you got. Also out front, close to the house, stay away from too much blue! How about daffodils and tulips? Now's the time. Consider yellow, reds, pink. Maybe a box in front of the basement window—or just plant it and be done. Shovel doesn't seem to go very deep before hitting rock, gravel.

Out back, plant cabbages and chards; fill in the Virgin Bed with hardy, sun-handling thymes. Plant blue irises and some other bulbs back there, like crocus? Something for early spring? Then—say, a month from now—gird your loins and crowbar up the orange logs as Kris told you to, over a month ago! Rip out weeds. Call for a truckload of compost. Wait, first buy a wheelbarrow! Does there exist a super-small, no-big-deal lawn mower? Should it be grass or blue star creeper around little stone paths, that's the question.

Three beds left to plant, all mostly shade. Especially under the dogwood and the blue spruce. What'll it be? Bleeding heart? God, there's a plant whose name has new meaning for me now. However, it does thrive in shade.

I love a sleeping house. Be accurate: this house, when everyone's in it, healthy and safe. Hannah, T, and the cat.

August 6

Slipped out of bed very early this morning, already torn by indecision. Should I write or go to the garden? Just then I heard Hannah stirring upstairs, getting ready to come down and leap into our bed. What kind of mother is it who sneaks out of the bedroom, gardening clogs hooked in two fingers, in the chill (yes, a lovely early morning hint of fall), knowing full well that the child is about to leap onto the bed and wake up the lovely insomniac man with the scar down his chest and sore back muscles?

August 8

Went to White Oak Farm a few days ago with Kris. The owner is a tall, blond beauty in a great straw hat. She's from Gainesville, Florida, and told us that her whole life, as she's moved, even through the college years, she's brought along her favorite exotic plants—the way, it occurs to me now, some people hang on to their grandmothers' heirloom quilts. Near the end of the visit, we discovered a tiny orchid house, and in it, a shy, gentle fellow— the beauty's husband! At first he barely spoke. Then we asked him about his orchids, and he came to life. Intensely passionate. All trace of shyness gone, just like that.

In the end I bought four saffron bulbs, fall-blooming, for fifty cents each. I like their little red tongues.

August 10

Two nights ago, T had terrible nausea and vomiting, and a much more acute form of the back pain he's had since the surgery. We went to the emergency room at about 2 AM., and a few hours later they did an ultrasound and discovered gallstones, one of them quite big. At the scheduling desk we ran into T's cardiologist, and he said, in his wry, nonchalant way, that this sometimes happens after major surgery, especially if you lose a lot of weight very quickly. This was indeed T's story—thirty-five pounds in one week. The doctor put his hand on T's back, gave him a friendly pat.

"Man," he said, "after what you've been through, this'll be a piece of cake."

August 15

Woke up very blue and stiff in my spirit, hard to get out of bed. Katia and T were sleeping soundly in the morning sun, two days after gallstone surgery. It went well, and T's mysterious back pain is gone, but I can't seem to shake this paralyzed feeling: what else "sometimes happens" after heart surgery? Even the sunlight on the bed held me down. Why get up? So many projects, but none of them yet ripe, or I am not ripe for them.

But I did finally get up. Put on an old white shirt and favorite old black flower-print cotton skirt, socks, and gardening clogs, and went out into the back garden. Cool and fresh; maybe fall is really coming. Fed the roses (I'm sure I'm hopelessly off schedule), deadheaded the butterfly bush, plucked a few cherry tomatoes, watered the jasmine vine and the window boxes, and started, as usual, imagining the garden's future. When I got back in, T was up and about. Still doesn't have his appetite back and is generally sore all over. (From the anesthesia, they told us. Expect it.) But he ate some cherry Jell-O and two crackers, and is ready to take a walk out to the university's cow barns. He is not letting this setback get to him. I won't let it get to me.

Later

M.F.K. Fisher's volume of journals, *Stay Me, Oh Comfort Me*, begins in 1933 with these three sentences:

> In the last three days, the currents have changed as many times. I feel them shifting all around me. It makes the thickness of a blue rug and the hard beauty of zinnias in a bowl seem more than ever things to feel and see.

She is still married to her first husband when she writes this. She doesn't know that she's on the cusp of enormous change: the Great Depression, the war, her falling in love with Dillwyn Parrish, his terrible illness and eventual suicide in the face of astonishing physical agony. But you can hear something in her voice already. She is going to live, by God. Not without rupturing the status quo, not without guilt, not without sorrow. But through all of this, her senses will be coming to life. She is going to pay close attention. She is going to be, as Henry James once said, "a person on whom nothing is lost."

Fall

Fall Planting

The shift toward fall in our lush Oregon valley is so slight you can't mention it out loud—you'd sound like a two-bit psychic. Besides, knowledge is always more satisfying if kept to oneself. The true beginning of fall in western Oregon is so cleverly self-concealing and elusive it deserves a good solitary savoring in the dark fertile mind.

I kept it to myself as long as I could, but the fact is, it came tucked into a run of hot early September days. I woke up one morning and saw, through the skylight over our bed, that the sky was a definitively darker blue than it had been the day before, and the big elm that looms out of the Newman Center courtyard, its branches waving like oracular wands, was a darker green than ever, ancient and sober and wise, with the gravitas of the last green of summer, weighty and full of shadows. On my morning walk I felt it again, barely, the intensified edge between two seasons.

I have been profligate, a connoisseur of seasons, desperate from the get-go for the savor of change. Growing up in Southern California, I always longed for more definite, obvious changes. And in early adulthood, as I moved from California to Iowa, then Boston, I was almost overwhelmed by the fulfillment of my wish: fall seemed a kind of orgiastic show: in-your-face hot colors and pungent smells of rotting apples, pumpkins, old flowers.

But here in Oregon, where it appears I have finally settled, I will have to learn to observe more subtly, more minutely, to catch the faint shift. I am being challenged by the place to use my senses, to bow down before the utterly complex maybe of this moment.

A few mornings later I thought the turn was undeniable. At the farmers' market, early in the morning, the farm-stand workers were wearing big jackets and gloves, winter hats. They looked stunned and sleepy, their roughened hands cold, slow to pile up leeks and onions, the tomatoes that came so late this year. "It took me by surprise," said one farmer. "It seems too soon." He pointed over to another stand, piled high with Asian pears, Transparent apples, corn in mounds, dried fruits, and filberts, and gazed at them with a mixed expression of pleasure and worry: "Look at that—it's really harvest time." But fifteen minutes later, their gloves were off, jackets too, and the warm sunlight was back. There was no more talk, that day, of the coming rains. It was as if we'd all forgotten.

Still, like Eve having bit the apple, I knew now where we were headed. It took me a few days to absorb the truth that the fall was here—or, more rightly, for the truth to absorb *me*. But soon enough I found myself squatting mercilessly beside the bolting arugula, pulling it out with a certain mournful violence, a form of acceptance, I suppose. In the next instant I found myself looking numbly at the great empty patches I'd created among the last—but still blooming— dahlias and delphiniums and coreopsis and lavender, all in fine fettle and not suffering in the least. I admired their attractive careless sensuality. We're not done yet, they seemed to say. Nowhere near done.

The mixed feeling wouldn't go away. It craved resolution, or at least action. Trancelike, I made my way to various nurseries around the county, first to absolve myself of the arugula crime. I brought home starts of Bright Lights chard, mustard greens, and more arugula. Also two kinds of cabbage, the purple and the green. Another handful of saffron crocuses, fall-blooming, their little red tongues so alluring on the package label. The next day I planted, and was granted a few minutes of contentment.

But soon my restlessness was back. My mind raced past the anxious melancholy of fall, vaulted over hibernatory winter and the time of rain, rain, and more rain, leaped over this as over the February muds of our region, to true early spring, for which we should be planting now. It is the right and natural thing to be doing, so why does it feel indecent?

Soon enough I succumbed to the next feeling. I went back to a local garden shop and bought bulbs: narcissus and Dutch iris and tulip, and a candytuft for that early look of cascading snow in March, here in the Willamette Valley, where our rare snows never last long. I went further still: to that grand dame of local nurseries, Garland, a few miles out of town and across a set of railroad tracks, with its vast array of alphabetized herb-and-perennial tables, its canopy of shade cloth over hellebores and ferns, the separate greenhouses for annuals, tropicals, vines; oh, even a backroom full of bonsais, where a mysterious hush prevails, broken only by the occasional ghostly clack of a bamboo chime.

Once I got there, I was further seduced. Over my head flapped special banners: Fall is Planting Time! Yet the place was suspiciously empty. In the giftshop and out near the birdbaths, the great wood-and-metal wind chimes sang out to no one. Two nursery employees nudged my cart to the side of the path; it was *their* season now, and I'd intruded after-hours. Such desolation! The little sale! signs had fallen on their sides, and several yarrows were tipped over, as if after a wild midsummer debauch. And yet, the contradiction remained: in the annuals house, barrels overflowed with tulip bulbs, with special deals and vivid cardboard displays.

Where was everybody?

It dawned on me slowly, this truth I'd decided to embrace: maybe I'd been privileged to hear the sounding of the bell early. I held my little secret close, and gathered up my store of goods. The banners waved in the sharp, new mountain air, alive with a tang of distant snow. Behind me, a hundred wind chimes cried in magical lonely chorus—*attend to me, attend to me*—like the coming autumn itself.

Gardener's Journal

This morning, a land use planner from Portland telephoned to say that they "want to work" with us as they develop a plan for "the Newman Commons" next door. We are devastated. We'd heard faint rumors back in late August, but we didn't know where the rumors had originated, and they seemed to us fantastical: who could imagine bulldozers taking down such a beautiful, established set of Craftsman houses and trees? Well, we'd said to each other, if it really turns out to be true, we'll fight it, that's all.

There followed a long silence, in which no new rumors surfaced, and we convinced ourselves that we'd gotten alarmed for nothing. Then this phone call. As I listened to the planner, the fight fizzled out of me. Her pleasant, concerned tone made it worse, I think: like a doctor, telling you it's terminal.

We want to work with you. What does that mean, exactly? Will they save the great old trees? Will they keep the parking lot from being either too big or right up against our back fence?

They're not evil. We just don't want those lovely old houses and trees to disappear. They're planning to tear everything down, and make one four-story, block-long brick building, with retail on the ground floor and sixty-four student apartments above. Parking lot where the courtyard is now, abutting our back garden.

Must call the Historical Preservation Advisory Board about the houses, and someone in city planning about the fate of the trees.

A friend just called and said, "You'll be a domestic island!"
There was a faint hint, in his voice, of *we told you so.*

The fear that we can't save this place makes me want to take
photographic portraits of the block. Maybe we can get a tour of
the interiors of the Newman Center houses. We've never been
inside. I want to photograph the courtyard, too. The last few nights,
I've heard a baby crying back behind us in one of the houses.
Every evening, around eight, she cries for an hour, then ceases.
The trees wave over our heads. The baby cries. A car sweeps past.
I am not ready to lose all this. They keep telling us that the houses
were "let go" from back in the sixties, that it would cost too much
to renovate them. But how did it happen, we wonder, that such
charming, potentially historic buildings were "let go" in the first
place? This seems a mystery.

Also I should go inside the courtyard itself, and find out what
other trees are back there, what kind of shape they're in. I especially
need to know the health of the big elm whose branches wave in
our skylight, gold-lit wands in late September. There's a young aspen
back there too, right at the fence. And very close to the big elm, a tall
fir whose branches look spindly and dry, clearly not in great shape.
Today T plans to call the city's Planning Commission, to see if there's
anything we can do.

September 25

Walked around the neighborhood on a surprisingly cold afternoon
with our neighbor Peggy Dearing and another woman who lives
a few blocks away, an oceanographer named Carol. Hannah came
along for a while, perking up whenever cats were present—I have
neglected to say that Katia has been the love of her life since we got
her, and puts up with all sorts of squeezing and hugging. Anyway,
after an hour in the chill air, I took Hannah home. She went into
the little annex in her bedroom she calls her "reading closet" with
The Cat from Nowhere, and I went back out with the women. Flashes

of village life as we walked with our clipboard and leaflets, and a new recognition of what an interesting neighborhood we inhabit: the students living in casual near-squalor, and just a few families left on these blocks near campus, including a young couple with a two-year-old daughter (the father was out with the daughter at a football party, and the young wife had "exactly two hours" to clean house and start a craft project, she said, laughing). The old professor next door wasn't home, so we left a leaflet inside his screen door and stopped at the next house, which belongs to an artist and her companion. I kept getting distracted from the task at hand and wanting just to look at their living spaces, to get a sense of the inhabitants' personalities from the objects in each house. There's the Dearings' place, for instance, so thick with life in the form of papers, books, their two young sons' school artwork, old china and mementos. The artist's house was as intensely spare as the Dearings' was rich in artifacts. Everyone has a different form of cocooning.

September 28

I thought I'd gotten ahead of the game. That is, I'd planted everything I'd bought for my new garden, and was content. I could stop for a while, maybe clean the bathroom, at least until I got my nerve up to tackle the lower terrace (sounds so upper-class, doesn't it?). But the garden doesn't want you to stop, and it will use your friends to get what it wants. How else to explain the coincidence? Within twenty-four hours I received two spontaneous visits from my gardening friends, Kris and Martha. Kris came first; she is of Scandinavian stock, in her mid-fifties and about six feet tall, her bearing as regal as a Magus'—a resemblance only heightened by the soft, dark-blue head cloth she's been wearing since her chemotherapy in June. And like one of the Magi, she came bearing gifts: a cardboard box full of iris rhizomes, freshly divided, from her yard. Not an hour later, Martha materialized in the backyard: elegant and tomboyish at once, with her short, glossy auburn hair and lean runner's limbs, her two young sons trailing behind. She was cradling a box of four infant honeysuckle vines she'd propagated herself. She only had a minute, as she was taking her boys to soccer practice, but we stood briefly together at the chain-link fence on the north side of the house, where she held out one slim arm, conductor-like, to direct my attention to the weedy, neglected stretch of hard dry earth at its base.

"One honeysuckle can go there," she said. "Another there, and so on." Then, like Mercury, she was gone, leaving me one step closer to that vision of the lush green wall of scent.

I love directness in a friend, the command a breathless, perhaps dying form. Authority is crucial when you give a garden gift: you must know where it goes; you must override any terror the novice has. So in honor of these two friends I held off writing and went back to the garden, to the hardest dirt of my little world thus far. Discovered a new technique: the sideways slicing hack. Added planting mix, hacked some more. Got the honeysuckles planted at last. Martha always has this effect on me: time is of the essence! Anyway, they sit very tenderly now in their little homemade soil bundles.

Kris seemed, at first, a little less urgent about the irises. She said, "Take your time. Some of these have been lying on concrete for three years, and they're still okay, the poor little guys." But that last phrase! I'll feel guilty until I get the last one in, doubtless years from now.

September 30

Two bad dreams. One in which Hannah cried terribly because I told her a story about herself, beginning with "When Daddy and I were together." In the dream she told me it was because I had said this that she was so upset. It was as if she could no longer stand to be reminded. She was inconsolable, in a way that I have not seen for over a year now. I realized, waking up, that I am always secretly braced for a storm.

In the other dream, a former student of mine who has always spooked me, a guy with several learning disabilities and a rough temper who seems to have been at the university as long as I have, never leaving, and always, always appearing when I step into the Memorial Union for lunch, this guy was up in Hannah's room, waving at me as I stood below on the back porch. I thought, *Now, this has gone too far,* and I grabbed him by the shirt collar as he was coming out of our house and said, "Come with me to the coffee shop, we have to talk." I had just bought him a cup of coffee and set it down on the table, ready to tell him to stop it, when I woke up.

Later

This morning there were beautiful narrow yellow leaves blowing all over the back deck and garden, and a haze over the blue sky, not a summery hot choky haze but a fall cooling, a faint coastal mistiness. The Pacific is just over those hills—it's easy to forget. Planted three narcissi in the Virgin Bed, made coffee, and came back upstairs to my study to write, and to read Charles Saunders's *Under the Sky in California.* How beautiful it must have been down there in 1913. Makes me sad. I take in the heft and appetite of the words themselves, vanishing fast from the landscape of my birth: *mesa, chaparral, chamise, potrero, cañada, cienega, rincon, arroyo, tule.*

    Rincon: a place where two hills come together to form a corner or nook.

October 1

Ripped out bee balms, for they were wracked by powdery mildew. Kris was sanguine: just cut them back, try again next year. Martha shook her head. Ugh, she said, I'd get rid of them. I'm afraid this is my inclination, too, though I love their rampant self-sowing habit, the spiky bright red and pink and purple—they're so full! But triage it was, in the end. Goners.

    Planted some of Kris's irises. Put some of them, and some narcissi, too, in the bee balms' place, and in the spot where the two peppers never took. The iris box seems bottomless, though. Gardened without gloves—it felt so good, all that dark, aged soil. Satisfying.

October 2

Bought a dreamy old bicycle yesterday: a blue women's "Columbia Roadster," sold by an old man who chains bikes to a lamppost on Harrison Boulevard now and then. You take the price tag and go knock on his door, around the corner. Thirty-five bucks for this beauty—the wire basket I bought that afternoon cost more than the bike! This morning I rode it out to the farmers' market at the county fairgrounds. It seems like we should be nearing the end of harvest season, but in fact we have a good two months yet. The last farmers' market, the one I find most beautiful and haunting, is held the week before Thanksgiving. Hardly anyone will be there, and the vendors themselves will be bundled up in bulky parkas or sheepskin vests, selling mostly apples, squashes, and the last tomatoes, which have lost the shocking juicy red of summer and are a timid, tired pink.

We're not there yet, but you can feel it coming. I see it in the cold hands of Flora, the Vietnamese farmer. What does she sell at this time of year? Okra! A lovely surprise—I planted some myself, but too late, I think. T and I will gobble it up: memories of living and teaching in Gainesville, Florida, for me, and of childhood Oklahoma summers for him. We can't get enough. Also French prunes, Asian pears, broccoli, snow peas, eggplant, and a crate of dark purplish-red round fruits with green stems. They look like a cross between an eggplant, a beet, and a plum—what are they? I must find out next time, and also ask her the names of other things. I could watch Flora's face all day; she reminds me of Mrs. Rodriguez, the housekeeper who worked for my mother for more than thirty years, a woman I came to think of as my true grandmother. Nana, I called her when I was little. She's in her early nineties now, still living in her own house in Alhambra, east of Los Angeles. Like Mrs. Rodriguez, Flora has a kind, deeply lined face and clear eyes full of calm good humor. She wears, intriguingly, a surgical glove on her right hand, so I can only see the left: small, tanned, and work-roughened, the fingers thickened and wrinkled, and numb with cold today. But she doesn't fumble at all. With great care and delicacy, she lifts a cold silver dime out of her gray change tray and puts it into my palm.

October 6

From Vivian Gornick's book of essays *The End of the Novel of Love,* a quote that matches exactly T's descriptions of depression. He hasn't had a deep bout of it for a few years now—the last one was just before his own divorce, five years ago—but it lives in him always, a constant blue humming presence, and we've been told by just about everyone, from doctors to friends, that half of all men who have heart surgery go through a terrible deep depression at some point. So, in some obscure way, I suppose we're both waiting. When will it come? The quote comes from the essay "Clover Adams," as prelude to the suicide of Clover, wife of Henry Adams. I put it here as a reminder to myself of its reality, that grief and fear hibernate, at best, in our lives and homes, even on days of joy and ease, and to be mindful of it always, hold it in one palm, the joy in the other, balanced, weighed together. This would seem strange, I suppose, but in my marriage I did not look or listen long enough, hard enough. I believed in the surface joy and liveliness my husband and I shared, and didn't question how much of our lives we kept separate from each other. I believed in the lovely shared times the way one might believe in the broad surface of a big river, when in fact even beneath the flattest surface there are holes and rocks shifting the currents all the time, changing the nature of the stream itself, silently, beneath. It suited me to believe all was well, and I did not pay attention. I am only now beginning to see, faintly, what is required. Gornick writes:

> In any life, the doubts, the depressions, the absence of self-belief—
> if not engaged with—progressively worsen, moving ineluctably
> from occasional ailment to recurrent episode to chronic
> condition. The condition occupies space, eats up air, consumes
> energy. Energy that should have fed experience now feeds the

unlived life. The unlived life is not a quiescent beast. The unlived life is a little animal in a great rage, barely permitting of survival. And sometimes not even that. Sometimes, it ends an assassin.

Two nights ago Hannah asked me which house I liked better: this one or Daddy's. I tried to stay neutral, quiet, though I felt, powerfully, the old terror and guilt. Is this Clover Adams's "little animal in a great rage"? A wave of fear gathered in me, a big one. But I tried to hold on, ride it the way I rode the crests of labor contractions during Hannah's birth, tried to remember that this was her question, her moment. I pressed myself to stay there: look into her eyes, listen, leave an opening for her to say whatever she needed to say, no matter what it was. To remember that the crisis of separation would never end for her, would only go dormant, rise again, sleep, and wake.

I kept my answer simple, short. I told her that while it was true I loved this house very much, I loved the old one, too—it's a beautiful house. She gave out a great sigh, and I felt the gates opening: those necessary, frightening gates. She began to list all the wonderful things about the other house: the bay window in the kitchen, the tulip tiles, "and to tell you the truth, Mom, it's more organized."

And to tell you the truth. I felt the pain and the hurt imbedded in that phrase. It's amazing how quickly the visceral experience of those first days of separation return. When I let myself go there, the color of each room rises before me: peach living room, yellow dining room, Hannah's salmon-colored closet. My husband holding his head in two hands, and my own hands horribly empty, as if they've just let go of a fragile bowl. Both of us side by side on the back porch, under a bright full moon. At last able to breathe, to talk. But just barely.

Upstairs, at bedtime, Hannah was less anxious, but something still troubled her. She said, "I like the funny wallpaper, and the two square rooms we made, but there's still something that's not quite me. Too much color, too many posters." Then, with marvelous speed, she said she wanted a purple shelf over her head, with a lamp to read by (very reasonable) and a red closet. Color! Then, gulp, she said she wanted her walls "color-washed" like the dining room at Dad's house. Oh! I had hoped to put behind me some of the things that distract me from writing. What am I facing here? Can I ever satisfy that longing, that loss of hers?

I don't know that I can. But I want to try. I want her to feel she has a warm, inviting room.

I'd better do it soon. Am I being too indulgent?

More of Clover Adams, who haunts me. Her own words this time, after visiting a gallery in New York. They were written in the mid-1880s, only months before she will kill herself.

> I saw there a superb old Chinese dish, jade color—tracery under the dull glaze—about two feet in diameter and turned up at right angles, a brim about three inches, deliciously modelled, made beyond everything for five lily pads and four white lilies—one hundred and seventy-five dollars. I don't wish to put so much money in anything so easily broken, but it is hauntingly fascinating.

She sounds so much like M.F.K. Fisher: the simple, keen observation, with the word "deliciously" slipped in, and in the envelope made by a pair of dashes, she heightens our suspense—tracery under the dull glaze—and barely betrays her pleasure. But, unlike Fisher, she rebukes herself, or the object, before surrendering one last time to the pleasure it gave her. Or is it something deeper, darker than pleasure? For it still holds its full mystery back from her.

October 8

Found on my pillow, this afternoon, Naomi Shihab Nye's new book of poems, *Fuel*. T must have bought it at Grass Roots, our sweet old independent bookstore, downtown. I loved finding the book on the pillow, a silent, unremarked gift. Reminds me of our early days (I love to refer to them so; sounds like some historical thing), when a book would appear out of nowhere, Terrence Des Pres's *The Survivor*, or *Nothing but You: Love Stories from "The New Yorker,"* or *The Great Works of Jewish Fantasy and Occult.* T said later he bought this book because of a particular poem. I knew immediately which one it was.

My Friend's Divorce

I want her
to dig up
every plant
in her garden
the pansies
the pentas
roses
ranunculus
thyme and lilies
the thing nobody knows
the name of
unwind the morning glories
from the wire windows
of the fence
take the blooming
and the almost-blooming
and the dormant
especially the dormant
and then
and then
plant them in her new yard
on the other side of town
and see how
they breathe

October 10

This morning, after taking Hannah to school, I came back, scrubbed out the shower (Why do I avoid it so? Only took ten minutes), and planted the rest of the narcissi. Put most of them in the Virgin Bed, but also plunked some down in—what shall we call it, the Most Sun

Bed? I socked 'em in between the dahlias and the okra (soon to go, I feel certain) and behind the cabbages, for surely in March there will be nothing but mud there. Seems impossible, hard to imagine forward to the different pleasure that must be taken from a single green stalk rising out of a mud pie, then a scattering of yellow, white, and pale orange in early spring. I'm thinking now, impulsively, of some radically red and pink tulips in a planter or two, for an April surprise.

I became aware, as I planted, of the change in the light. I know it's been happening all month, but I failed to notice it. Today, I thought, why not keep a record? Very unscientific of course, but something nonetheless. Let's use the Virgin Bed as the marker:

9:15: only the top third of the Shrine itself is in sunlight.

There's my science for the day. No wonder the tomatoes aren't happening anymore. Going to have to put next year's along the fence in front of the Most Sun Bed. And start them earlier. I am enchanted by the idea of *cold frames* and *cloches,* as much for the sound of the words as for their function. And it's nice to think of starting early.

Later

I love walking among the students on campus this fall, going to the occasional committee meeting. I dress nicely for these, even though I am on leave for the term, and not teaching. I stroll from our house to the Honors College very slowly. Students in bright fall sunlight, swerving madly on their bikes, or late to class, running. Someone is selling posters of rock musicians on the quad, and big clusters of friends develop and split, develop and split. They all seem intensely social right now, beginning of the year, lots of greeting cries and dramatic hilarity. Makes me think, obscurely, of squirrels and birds in their last frantic fall gathering and play. Things will get quieter in November, when the rains begin, but now, in October, there is still a lively chattering. I know this pleasure is a luxury; what I really love is the chance to walk among them anonymously, without having to stride into a classroom the next minute and stand before them, all tweedy and mock-stern, bespectacled authority, though this too has its pleasures—the pleasures of the masque.

October 12

A twilight trip to the covered bridge and the cow barns last night; a sky full of hectic pink clouds, and Hannah in shorts, a fuzzy purple fleece and purple skates, with those summer-brown legs beautifully long and fragile-looking as she pushed forward on the path. She tugged wildly on our arms, but T was utterly calm no matter what. And me? Losing it! Wanting to listen to the frogs, the trees, silence. She was absolutely full of pepper, that girl, wouldn't stop talking for a minute, and I thought, *My mother would laugh to see this.* I was apparently the same way: impossible to shut up. T rescued me later; played catch with Hannah in her room before bed, while I went to the piano and practiced the little "Passepied," by Bach. This helped calm my feeling of chaos. But I dreamed, toward morning, that I was sick unto dying, and our family doctor came to see me (I was in a room I didn't recognize) and told me that his daughter was dying, too. Somehow I understood that he was comforting me because my own father couldn't be there, and I hoped there was someone there for his daughter. God, I was sick! It felt really awful, like a very long bad cold with fever, etc. Pneumonia? During the dream itself, I had physical sensations of being ill: fever, aches, exhaustion. What do you make of that?

The dream of sickness has made me dig out my recipe for Chicken Noodle Soup Tonkinoise.

I must acknowledge my two sources and inspirations. First: my mother, of course. She loves to call chicken soup "Jewish penicillin," and, with all the pride of a former dietitian, occasionally reminds me that its healing powers have been scientifically proven. But what I remember is the way, when I was young, she would put a bowl of it, gleaming with jewels of fat, on a little TV tray and let me watch extra cartoons.

Second: On Ninth Street, there's an Asian grocery with a few tables, called Little Saigon, run by a woman named Vonnie Pham. She makes an ambrosial chicken stock, with a depth of spice I don't usually associate with chicken broth but is wondrous; I am never going back to the old bland European way. Star anise is involved, as are cloves and sugar. I asked Vonnie her secret, and she began by bringing out a little red box from the shop shelves: *Gia Vi Nau Pho PASTEUR Chinese special spice "pour Soupe Tonkinoise."* The ingredients of the filter bag are as follows: fennel, star anise, coriander, cinnamon, cloves, and sugar. But I think you could just get these whole spices and tie them up in a little cloth bag, and drop it into the soup pot. (On the box there's a recipe for the soup, and it says "ginger and onion (burn them)." Yes: a fast sauté to bring out their flavors.

Ingredients for stock:

Chicken backs and necks—two for greater depth
A couple of carrots
An onion cut in half, but unpeeled
A few broken cloves of garlic, unpeeled
Several slices of unpeeled ginger
The white parts of two or three lemongrass stalks, smashed or cut a little
A teaspoon or two of kosher salt and a scattering of peppercorns
Whole spices in bag: fennel, star anise, coriander, cinnamon stick, cloves
Sugar, a couple teaspoons at least (could do this later, when you make the soup itself)

Do a quick sauté of the garlic and ginger before throwing them into the pot. Bring the stock to a boil, skim off the scum, simmer, covered, for an hour or a little more. Another dark secret here: like my mother, Vonnie doesn't skim off the fat. So, up to you! She serves hers with tender chicken-thigh meat, sliced green and regular onions (also "burnt" first), and rice noodles. At the very end of the cooking, add a teaspoon or two of Vietnamese fish sauce (*nam pla*). Go easy: it's potent and very salty! Add your sugar.

On the side, a plate of limes, Thai basil, and Thai peppers.

Hannah slurps this soup down, sans peppers. Though the intensity of the flavor is in part due to the keeping of the fat, I am skimming it off at home. It looks quite different to me since T's heart surgery. Though he's recovering beautifully, quite slim and cholesterol levels nice and low, we don't need to tempt fate with chicken fat.

October 13

Gardenish matters: Today I bought a number of dark-leaved things, not unlike my new dark olive sweater—it's getting harder to write without wearing that sweater, oh dear! But the dark-leaved things: Jack Spratt flax and something else whose tag I've already lost—a chocolaty evergreen grass from Australia, to go, along with Japanese blood grass, beside the two Red Heart Rose of Sharon shrubs, which Martha, not long ago, dubbed "the bloody-tissue plant" for the way the petals look when they drop. Marvelous. Where did *that* come from, I asked her, laughing. She thought for a moment, then remembered a book she'd read recently on Western pioneer women. Turns out the author refers, at one point, to a particular Rose of Sharon that the women described as "white with bloody centers." Must be this very one, she said.

And added, with a wicked smile, "We are so very primitive, aren't we?"

Not done yet. Also bought a couple handfuls of crocus bulbs and a dark red-brown glazed pot, very Asian-looking, with a maidenhair fern to go in it, for the dining room, which we want, someday, to paint a deep handsome red.

Luscious dark, the fall, my favorite season. It is a dark broth season, copper-colored, with the last green leaves filtered between and a few hot yellows left here and there. Sensual and elegiac.

Last week, the architects and land-use planners for the Newman Commons came to our door. They would not, at first, come inside (one is very allergic to cats), so T and I met them on the sidewalk in front of our house. I ran back inside for my notebook, and carried it with me the whole time. I was aware of clutching it, and aware, too, that I wanted the developers to notice it in my hands.

Almost immediately, the assistant architect began to shoot photos of our house, of the street, of the apartment complex directly across the street, its flat façade, its barren sidewalk and parking strip, the small parking lot behind Young's Kitchen, a Korean restaurant catercorner to our house. He looked like a detective after a crime, though I feel like he was gathering the evidence *before* a crime. One of the other visitors remarked on the noise and traffic on Twenty-first Street, and this, too, seemed a kind of proactive move, as if to say, Listen, you already live in an urban area, with a three-story apartment building across the street. How can you object to another?

Or: Let's be honest, how can the city Planning Commission object? There is already a precedent.

Nonetheless, we said what we've said before, and feel: that despite everyone's warnings to us about living so close to campus and "all those students," we'd been pleasantly surprised at the relative quiet of our street, which is primarily a pedestrian path to campus. Just as we said this, the garbage, recycling, and plant-refuse trucks rolled up, one after another.

"Whoa," said the land-use planner.

"It's trash day," I replied.

They took us inside the Newman Center's main building, the house called Hillside, and showed us the blueprints for the project. I wanted a full tour, wanted to explore its bay windows and Craftsman nooks and crannies, but they directed us to a meeting room, very businesslike. We want to be good neighbors, they said. We want to enhance, not destroy, your experience of living here. A couple of good things were promised: a ten-foot-wide "green barrier" between our house and their parking lot, even a pergola to grow roses on, to echo, said the architect, the Craftsman details of our house. The small parking area south of our house would also be converted to "green." I suggested a community garden there, or perennial beds, and offered to help if they went that way. They seemed interested in that, but I doubt they'll go for a community garden plot; it won't fit with the glass-and-brick four-story building they're planning.

We went with them into the courtyard, where the parking lot would go. Where the great trees are, the elm and fir whose branches and leaves filter the western light into our garden and kitchen and bedroom all afternoon, so beautifully, so variously, all year long. This is our biggest fear, for what developer would create a parking lot with the idea of saving trees? The more I looked, the more I saw how denuded the future might be. It's not just those two big ones behind our house that will go, but the mature maples on Monroe, and some others behind the Dearings' backyard. The parking lot will have to cover a big area, to accommodate not only the sixty-four apartments but people coming over for worship services and other activities, as well as to their proposed "cybercafé." "We're looking to create a faith-based community," they said.

What did people used to say, before this euphonious phrase gained currency?

"But all those trees," we murmured.

The assistant architect, the one with the camera, said, "We're really not at the stage where we can fine-tune the plan." This, after just showing us a detailed blueprint of the building and parking lot. What, then, is fine-tuning?

Before they left, we took them inside our house, minus the allergic land-use planner, who went around to our side gate to wait in the back garden. First we took them upstairs, into Hannah's room, to show them how little privacy she'd have from the windows of the apartment complex, as she grows into young womanhood. Then back downstairs, into our bedroom. I pointed to the skylight over the bed, and said, "If you lie down, you can get the full effect of the tree in the skylight."

Of course nobody took me up on it. What was I thinking?

In the garden, they exclaimed over the dahlias, the mosses and blue star creeper and the Don Juan climbing rose. It is easy to be complimentary about gardens: but will it make a difference in the decision about the last great trees of our neighborhood?

One of them said, "We'll plant new ones."

I shook my head. "We'll be dead before they get as big as these."

"True," he said. "True."

After they were gone, I called Kent and Trish, Kris's in-laws and former city commissioners. Kent thinks the old buildings might qualify as historical, and that there might be something we can do with "neighborhood compatibility and scale." Another friend, in the city's public works department, says if the trees are on their property, we haven't got a prayer.

Why does this story already feel written? The planners were so cavalier about the old cottages. Standing in our yard, looking at them, the chief architect said, "The construction won't take long. Some of these things look like if you breathe on them too hard, they'll fall over."

October 17

From the final two pages of M.F.K. Fisher's journal *Stay Me, Oh Comfort Me*. This epilogue was written many years after the death of her second husband, Dillwyn Parrish, and her own departure from Bareacres, the place they bought together in Hemet, California, out in the Southern California desert. She suggests that we need to see clearly what is, what has always been, inevitable on this planet, even as our recognition of the truth is buried by our powerful need to hope. For she is never without hope, and that is why I find her so great. If we are lucky enough to discover love, we will inevitably discover grief. If we are granted a taste of paradise, we will see it changed by the forces all around us. The fight matters, but there is no winning. Only ask of yourself a greater curiosity, a deeper, more potent generosity of observation. Anyway, her combination of melancholy courage and acceptance and fierce appetite for whatever's next is the thing that matters.

I am told that the fine pure air that first drew us there, half mountain and half desert, is now foul with smog and that the rich carpet of fruit trees we looked down on is solid with RVs and trailer parks. One block on Main Street is now in the Guinness Book of World Records, or maybe it is Ripley's Believe It or Not: something like 182 banks and savings-and-loan offices on that sleepy little stretch of sidewalk! And there are almost a hundred doctors, most of them connected with "convalescent homes" of varying status and opulence. And Crest Drive is lined with million-dollar villas with the subdivision where Bareacres was ("a ninety-acre hell of red-hot rocks and rattlesnakes," as one New Yorker described it to us after a lost weekend there) the most snobbish and stylish area between Palm Springs and Los Angeles.

That is the way it is, and I do not grieve or even care . . . I have taken and been given more than can ever be known that is heartwarming and fulfilling forever from that piece of wild haunted untillable land we named Bareacres for a time. No doubt roads have been cut into it and rocks have been blasted away, but I know that the contours cannot change much in a few hundred years in that country. And meanwhile the ghosts are there, even of the sick sad Indians who went to lie in the magic lithium waters of the spring, and even of the poor squawman with a bullet in his heart, and of my own mother who loved the place . . . they are all there to cleanse and watch over it. . . . There are many pockets of comfort and healing on this planet, and I have touched a few of them . . .

—Glen Ellen, California, 1984

Word-Music

"There are many pockets of comfort and healing on this planet," Fisher wrote.

And, I want to add, some of them aren't physical spaces at all, but gifts given into your hands by a teacher who has, herself, the gift of deep attention. Gifts that send you on a journey that moves secretly through your life. Only in retrospect can you see the small back channel of the broader river, the one you can actually wade, the one you've been unconsciously following all along.

I'm thinking of my first college English teacher, who lent me a handful of books to grow on: some Virginia Woolf, a smidgen of E. B. White—and, after a slight pause, *A Death in the Family,* by James Agee. She hesitated, I think, because she knew there had been a death in my family, and didn't want to intrude. But she also knew that I wanted to write and was besotted with music. All this was probably clear from the simile-drenched essay I'd turned in, about my aunt's recent death from cancer. How else to express the mystery I'd felt in our guest bedroom as my aunt curved herself into a small shape on the bed and, the next moment, was gone? My teacher wisely said little. She told me to try again, without the similes, and to read Mr. Agee's novel.

Some books strike a double chord at once. We are caught not only by the story, but by the music of its telling: its rhythms, colors, and shape—and there is no separating the two. *A Death in the Family* overwhelmed me at eighteen, and still does, decades into a writing-and-teaching life. It is as much symphony as it is novel, from its elegiac overture, "talking now of summer evenings" in Knoxville 1915, to the scene in which the child Rufus encounters the desolate tenderness of the cosmos itself, "the nothingness" in whose very breath our small lives shelter. *A Death in the Family* taught me that music could have a life in prose, could bring a truth to life. That a word as small as *locust,* or *blue,* could shimmer and rise off the page.

What I didn't know—wouldn't know until a few years ago— was that in 1947, the American composer Samuel Barber was so deeply moved by Agee's words that he composed a musical setting of "Knoxville: Summer, 1915." His work for lyric soprano and orchestra, I soon learned, is as revered by music lovers as Agee's prose piece is by readers. And I didn't know, until the first time I listened to that work, how exquisitely two different art forms might fuse into one.

And so, though my own musicianship is primitive—a history of stops and starts at our family piano—I tried, not long ago, a small literary-musical experiment in my writing classroom. I was teaching *A Death in the Family* to a new crop of fiction writers at our university, and brought Barber's *Knoxville: Summer of 1915* along for the ride. One rainy afternoon, my students and I sat down at the seminar table with Agee's prose piece, Barber's score, and a small boom box. For the next hour, we abandoned our usual concerns of plot and character and listened to the startling affinity between two great artists, between one's music and the other's words.

Barber came upon Agee's "Knoxville" in the mid-1940s, in a ten-year anthology of the *Partisan Review.* He later recalled, "I had always admired Mr. Agee's writing and this prose-poem particularly struck me because the summer evening he describes in his native Southern town reminded me so much of similar evenings, when I was a child at home. . . . Agee's poem moved me deeply, and my musical response that summer of 1947 was immediate and intense. I think I must have composed *Knoxville* within a few days."

"My musical response," he said, describing a simultaneity of personal identification and aesthetic excitement. And when, in rainy Oregon, my students and I listened to the melancholy woodwinds give way to a kind of rocking motion, we heard that immediacy for ourselves—the braiding of Barber's rhythms and intervals and Agee's phrases. "It has become that time of evening when people sit on their porches, rocking gently and talking gently." From the beginning, the students caught on to a series of "pairings" or "doublings" in both the written phrases and the musical ones—and even, as one student said, a "rocking" between comforting memories and the apprehension of loss, of the dark night just beyond. We'd been talking all term about paradoxical images in literature, those images that sustain more than one meaning at once, and now the students heard the same phenomenon in music: at the top of a pleasant major chord, a grain of dissonance, of sorrow.

Both Agee's text and Barber's music are sometimes called nostalgic, but as my students and I discovered that afternoon, the word *nostalgia* doesn't do either of them justice. The power lies just beneath that easy rocking motion, beneath the lovely ease of a family spreading its quilt on the "rough wet grass."

Yet it's worth lingering on that initial homesickness as a threshold for these artists' complex shared poetry. When they first met to discuss the "Knoxville" collaboration, in 1947, they began to discover what Barber later called "odd coincidences" in their upbringing. He said, "We both had back yards where our families used to lie in the long summer evenings, we each had an aunt who was a musician. I remember well my parents sitting on the porch, talking quietly as they rocked."

The work has since gone on to be beloved of many great singers and conductors. Eleanor Steber, who debuted the work with Koussevitzky, told an interviewer, "It's my childhood, exactly!" and Leontyne Price once said, after recording it, "You can smell the South it in."

For a new generation of artists, the power of *Knoxville: Summer of 1915* may lie in a more twilight place. I've heard this from a young conductor I know, who was, like me, overwhelmed as a young man by the way the novel captured both the beauty and the terror of childhood. He says that this is the double feeling Barber caught so exactly: the comforting rocking motif of the beginning is still present, but in its inverted, sinister form, in the strident streetcar section, "raising its iron moan; stopping, belling and starting; stertorous;

rousing and raising again." But this section itself melts away into the sorrowful generous beauty of "now is the night one blue dew," and beyond it, into the climax, in which the speaker tenderly acknowledges the mortality of his family in its most peaceful hour. That prayerful section itself blooms into a child's wish to know who he is, and his simultaneous adult recognition that those who love him best, "will not, oh, will not, not now, not ever; but will not ever tell me who I am."

My students heard that culminating paradox: gratitude and sorrow and the unsolvable desire to know ourselves. This remains suspended, unresolved on the page. In the music, the rocking motion returns. But it too eventually floats off, suspended, into one last major seventh chord, one last lingering dissonance.

All these riches would have been enough, but there was to be one more gift: one of my fiction-writing students that year was also a soprano, taking voice lessons at the university. At her next lesson, she asked her teacher if she knew the Barber piece. "Of course," replied the teacher, taking the score from the top of her piano. "It's right here."

And so, through the rest of that rainy term, my student and I worked our way through the easier sections of the piece. I confess to a glimmer of nostalgia: I'll never hear it without seeing, in my peripheral vision, my student standing tall beside our family piano, waiting patiently for her entrance as I make my way through the stately, slightly dissonant chords of the introduction.

And I'll never hear it without remembering, too, that we are at the very piano my parents bought in 1975, the year of my aunt's death, in hopes of such a moment as this.

Gardener's Journal

This morning, at breakfast, Hannah asked me when the sun is due to explode, like other stars, and when it does, what will happen to us? I was thinking about the Newman Commons project, picturing the bulldozers and feeling bitter, ruffled, and small.

"Oh," I said, "we'll be long gone when that happens."

"What do you mean?" she asked.

"Well, people won't be here anymore," I said. "No species has lasted that long, and at the rate we're going—"

I heard myself, and stopped cold. Too late. She was very quiet, her eyebrows raised in surprise. I might as well have said, "We'll be blown up tomorrow, don't worry about lunch."

I tried to soften my voice and began to murmur some educational-sounding rot: how it wouldn't happen until "millions of years from now" and then "everything will start over again, bits of rock spewed out from the burning star, lava flows cooling, then the seas—"

Midway through, she calmly picked up her breakfast plate and carried it to the sink, all the while nodding absently.

It was more than I deserved.

October 19

Rough Draft of our letter to the Planning Commission. Will have to get city codes, etc., to send. But it's a start.

Corvallis Planning Commission
Corvallis Planning Division

Subject: Proposed demolition of the Newman Center and construction of Newman Commons, a four-story, sixty-four-apartment complex, chapel, Newman Center, and cybercafé.

Dear Planning Commissioners:
We live next door to the Newman Center. As immediate neighbors, citizens of Corvallis, and professors at Oregon State University, we strongly object to the Newman Commons project proposal. When we bought our house, we were influenced by its remarkable physical situation: on the university's doorstep, yet surrounded by the lush green sanctuary and historic atmosphere created by the Newman Center's Arts and Crafts–era architecture and landscaping. Although we made thorough inquiries with the city about potential changes to the neighborhood, there was no word on development of such a massive nature. We realize that by choosing to live in a campus-bordering neighborhood, we must be prepared for change, but we also feel, just as strongly, that older buildings, trees, and landscaping of historic value should be protected as the city develops, and that scale be given careful consideration. We have listed below, first, our main objections and, second, our specific concerns and suggestions for revision should the project be approved.

Historical and Environmental Concerns
As new members of this unique neighborhood, we object to the building project on historical and environmental grounds. The loss of the historic buildings and delightful green space on the university's

border is a loss that many will feel, both on campus and in the neighborhood. The destruction of Snell House in particular, with its classic Arts and Crafts architecture and historical significance, will be a loss for the city of Corvallis and Oregon State University. Dr. Margaret Snell was one of the first professional women in the state of Oregon and an early professor of home economics here. It is our deep sense that the Newman Center buildings and courtyards contribute a historic value to this campus-bordering neighborhood that is irreplaceable. We hope that measures will be taken to save Snell House.

Scale

The current proposal calls for a block-long, forty-five-foot tall building that is out of scale with the adjacent residential properties to the north and west. In the city of Corvallis's "Plan Compatibility Review," it is stated that a new building's size should be "in relationship to other buildings in the area" and that it should take into account the "character of surrounding development." Only a driveway stands between our property and the proposed building; thus the massive nature of the building should still be considered out of scale with our property and should not be more than one story taller than our house.

Solar Access

We urge the city to require solar maps with this plan. Without this information, it is impossible to tell whether "opportunities for use of solar energy [can] be protected." Furthermore, our property and particularly our back garden may suffer a severe loss of sunlight created by the shadows of a forty-five-foot-high, block-long building.

Privacy

Second floor: Our nine-year-old daughter's bedroom, on the second story of our house, will be directly exposed to the upper-story windows of the four-story apartment complex. We have discussed landscaping measures with both the project's architect and landscape designer, and while we appreciate their efforts, we are of course aware that whatever trees are planted, they will not reach a height to protect her from being viewed by the third- and fourth-story residents for the next seven years. Again, a revision of the plan showing two-story buildings on Monroe Street or on the alley would alleviate this problem. Should the current proposal be approved, however, we ask that building-design measures be taken to minimize views of her bedroom.

Trees and Landscaping

Parking lot/driveway area: We are grieved by the proposed removal of significant trees on the property that create a unique canopy in the neighborhood and affect our home and neighborhood environment, and ask that every effort is made to save as many of the big trees and plantings as possible.

To the best of our knowledge, the following trees and plantings require protection during construction:

A. Big-leaf maple in approximate middle of Newman Center property, close to the alley and Westminster House

B. Rhododendrons and smaller trees in "corner" directly behind our house and behind/adjacent to the neighbors' house.

C. In our yard: the blue spruce in our yard's southwest corner. This tree provides significant screening from the proposed building and parking lot, and it could be damaged if care is not taken during construction of the parking lot/driveway/ Newman Commons. It is of enormous concern to us that this tree, as well as the dogwood and all other trees on our property and on our neighbors' property to the north, be protected during and after construction, and that if any trees/plantings slated for protection are damaged, that the developers take full financial responsibility for replacement.

As professional writers and university professors, we'd very much like to remain in the neighborhood. The building of three- and four-story apartment complexes around us will inevitably drive families like ours out to the more suburban areas of Corvallis, creating a student ghetto around campus. While we are well aware of housing pressures in the student population, we also believe there is a value—for students as well as permanent citizens of this community—in sustaining a diverse population in campus and downtown neighborhoods. Our own home, of which we are only the third owners in nearly ninety years, is itself a fine example of Arts and Crafts interior design, and has been maintained handsomely through the years. Please help people like us stay in the neighborhood and keep Corvallis's history and charm alive as the city grows.

Thank you for your time and consideration.

Respectfully submitted,

October 22

Small pleasures: Hannah waking up at six-thirty, still in the dark, finding us at our desks. She curls up in an old armchair in my study with Katia in her lap, and watches me for a minute. Katia watches me, too. Both of them sleepy but alert with their big eyes, their delicately pointed chins.

"You look comfortable," Hannah says. "What are you writing?"

"A novel," I reply.

"Well," she says, "if you ever decide to write a children's book, let me know. I have lots of ideas."

The White Cat

In the stories you liked best as a child, my love, there was always a terrible repetition of tests. The hero, in order to win a wife and make his fortune, set out full of confidence to retrieve some object not even precious to himself. He was driven by the father-king who, facing the wobbling end of his reign, was in an unusually selfish, wheedling mood. And, let's face it, this father had never been a noble fellow: forever trying to steal a kingdom, or defend his own against imagined enemies.

Three times the hero plunges back into the unknown world he has by dream or accident discovered, where the treasure—coveted by the king, whose hungers are unconscious and therefore impossible to sate—lies surrounded by obstacle, tedium, dragon. Three times he plunges in; three times he risks his life to get the prize. First it's the golden apple, second, the magical linen woven of thread so fine the whole cloth can pass through the smallest needle, and, at last, the tiniest dog in the world, who can be heard barking inside a corn kernel, itself enclosed in a walnut shell.

The trouble is, in that other world, there appears someone more alluring than the object of the quest, for instance a beautiful white cat who begs the hero to stay—without words, of course. Please stay. Take the treasure back to the king, but come back. I need you here. I am forbidden to say why.

The mystery of the white cat's need, not to mention her startlingly human beauty and intelligence, is far more deep and fulfilling and morally necessary than the foolish king's demand for a golden something-or-other. It in fact makes the quest seem trivial, wrong, and inconsequential.

With each successive journey it gets harder and harder for the hero to cross the border back to the king, the real world. The reward—wife and land and future fortune—goes dim, the whole thing revealed for what it is, a repetitive, pointless exercise, an exchange of commodities: golden apple for king's kingdom, princess-bride, etc. With the taste of ashes in his mouth, the hero travels into middle age. Meanwhile, deep in the woods of his awakened imagination, the cat-queen who can offer no material reward or even a logical reason why he should give up the world for her waits helplessly by the midnight gates of her kingdom, bound by an ancient curse of silence, forbidden to ask favors or tell her story. Who is she? You don't know, but the prince's third and final return to his father's castle, with apple, linen, dog at last acceptable to the king, and the earthly reward achieved, always left you feeling hollow, incomplete.

By now the lost domain, with its caverns and balustrades, its pointed gates and absolute danger, had gotten hold of you.

Meanwhile, back in the king's palace, the elusive world is dismissed with shocking ease by courtiers and peasants alike. The prince himself is now bound by silence, too, his story trapped behind walls and briars and the hills in the distance, until, like the blurry cluster of the Pleiades, it is visible only when you gaze to the side.

But it's too late: your heart's been surprised, its true domain awakened. A domain that will haunt you until you go looking for it once more, on your own and without assignment, without hope that it will bring you anything useful in this world. Certainly it won't make your fortune. It will, in fact, destroy you, as far as the king and his courtiers are concerned. Is this the world you lean toward, the one you cannot reenter a fourth time without dying, without abandoning the life lived reasonably, dutifully, under the king? Do you fear that if you put your sword to that life, everything there, including the white cat, your silenced queen, might turn to ash along with everything here?

In the fairy tales of your childhood, my love, recall that the hero never came to this pass. He stayed home after the third journey, ever dutiful, and was rewarded by the last-minute appearance of a girl, strangely familiar, but from another kingdom entirely. And in that same moment, the father-king is released from the terrible grasp of his desires. Who can say which is the greater miracle? Never mind: the kingdom rejoices.

You rejoice too, but even at the height of celebration you suspect the truth. I do, too: I watch you sleeping. I know that when you look across the border in your dreams, you see her plainly there, the white cat lost in her castle, her woods, her kingdom, she of fantastic, inhuman dignity, forever awaiting rescue. Observe her closely. She is your own kerneled heart, woven of miraculous thread and thrice-protected from human view; she whose life will open like a palm on the day—please God, far from now—of your death. White cat, I am revealed for what I am: his human wife. Be patient. Keep by the gate as you must. Silent sufferer, cruelly bound, wait as we wait, but on the other side.

Gardener's Journal

October 23

We have picked our pumpkins out at Twedt's Farms, and strung our Halloween lights: red devils in the dining-room windows, and a combination of orange bats and violet Draculas with white heads in the living-room windows. T observes that the Draculas look like geishas. What are geishas? Hannah asks. Oh, Japanese dancing girls, we both say, very fast, and she gives us a tilted look, ever alert to what is left out. The lights, anyway, are nice late at night and even better very early in the morning when we perform—what does T call it?—*the grim ritual* of rising at five to write. When the rains come, they will be a great comfort, as will our bright red chili lights.

October 24

Hannah dreams of earthquake preparedness. In the dream, I'm sitting on her bed and she asks, "Do you know what to do in case of an earthquake?" I give an incomplete answer, something to the effect of "get under a desk." But then she quizzes me further: "And do you put your hands over your head?" Apparently I'm stumped by that one, can't answer. She also dreams that an old woman asks her for gardening advice, and she replies, "Ask my mom, she can make your garden last forever." A spooky pairing of dreams. Not surprisingly, she sees me as not entirely capable of protecting her. And I have my

79

own terrors of doing it badly. Does it matter that in her dreams, I can make a garden last?

I need to work on earthquake preparedness.

After I dropped her off at school—was I thinking of her dream?—I went into the garden with my bucket and clippers. I was wondering, in fact, if I could make the garden last till my mother gets here for Thanksgiving.

I gave it a good haircut all around, and we'll see. There are dahlias left in the back, and the Don Juan is in its last blooming of the fall, but best of all is the magnificent dogwood, in its autumn red, beautifully leaning to escape the ever-growing shadow of the blue spruce. The dogwood looks very Japanese. Its leaves blanket the garden along with yellows from somewhere—probably the elm, and also the young aspen just over the fence, another tree the developers want to cut down for the parking lot. In late fall, the intensity of the garden is not really in the flowers, but in the pattern of fallen leaves. I've never thought of it before, but if those trees go, that's another form of denuding. In the season when falling leaves are the beautiful thing, they'd be missing. Mostly mud.

Why it matters to me might be this: I can't describe, or evoke, what happens to me in fall, but it's the time when I have the most potent sensual awareness of the present. That's very abstract. Yet today in the garden, pouring the bucketful of old stems, finished blossoms, and yellow leaves into the big bin, I got a visceral *spang* of being alive. Something about the dense mix of colors, of heightened dark or bright. The wet leaves shine, as do the brown-tipped petals of the yellow and the salmon-colored dahlias, the burnt-brown seed heads of the Moonbeam coreopsis. I awaken, and my memory is hungry, as if it has an appetite of its own, dormant much of the time. I feel it as a sense now, operating inside me to collect and save the apparently inconsequential moment as I pass through it: grasping a hunk of the shriveled coreopsis blossoms in one orange-gloved hand. Snipping. Feeling the wet, cool air on my face as the first rain starts to fall. The little tapping of it on the big dahlia leaves, on the wood slats of the back deck stairs, and in the branches of the blue spruce. A faint rustling behind me as a few more leaves come down off the dogwood, red on the dark ground. Sharp tan needles under the spruce make a dry blanket, hiding the green of mosses and baby's tears just beneath. The smell of October rain, the fine coldness of hands.

October 26

Martha and I went out to a nursery on Highway 99, south of town. "Home Grown," it's called. She is great to shop with for plants—or anything else, for that matter. She is passionate and decisive, with a finely tuned authority. "Yes," she'll say, in a tone that means take it or you'll regret it forever. She also suggests wonderful ideas I sense are beyond me: planting shrubs asymmetrically, for instance. I'm not yet ready for real subversion. Yesterday she came over, and we stood in the driveway gazing together at the two "bloody-tissue plants" against the front of the house—she has forever changed the proper name of the plant for me; I'll never call it anything else. Anyway, these shrubs are naked and small just now, but are supposed to grow to a height of ten to twenty feet. Imagine a screen of white flowers rising up against the front windows; only when you get close do you see the droplet of red at their centers. Also, some other things: I tucked into a corner beside the front steps a drought-resistant gaura, and behind it, in another nook, a very young purple wisteria. Before she left, Martha warned, "Keep an eye on it. They've been known to take over, choke rain gutters."

After she was gone, I ripped the weeds out from the little blank space between ourselves and the north side of the Newman Center. They've said they'll make a pergola there. In my fantasies, I ask for, and get, a willow gate or a long archway with climbing roses. One can dream. But in any case, *something* will need to shield us from the changes next door. They look inevitable now.

On Our Streets

It was around this time last year that Junior died. We saw it in the town newspaper: "Police say homeless man was murdered." What did I know about Junior? Nothing, really. Why did so many people claim to know him? It surprised me at the time: someone would hear the news that he was dead and cry out, "I knew him." Inevitably the speaker would catch himself: "Well, I didn't really, but we used to talk whenever I saw him."

In the waning days of October, an impromptu shrine sprang up next to the post office entrance on Jefferson Street, where Junior went to get out of the rain. On the brick wall above the shrine someone taped up a photocopied snapshot of him. It must have been taken in winter: he wore his baseball cap pulled low over his eyes and a bulky patched coat. He smiled broadly at the camera, holding up two fingers in a peace sign. At the foot of the brick wall, where Junior used to hang out, people had laid small heaps of roses and dahlias and chrysanthemums, orange and yellow marigolds, too, the flowers popular on the Day of the Dead, their brightness and strong scent said to invite the spirits of our loved ones back to earth for a visit.

If he had come back, what else would he have seen? A single cigarette—the last one from his own pack, someone told me—and a flimsy restaurant matchbook. A single, foil-wrapped chocolate mint. Four tall prayer candles in glasses, and a cluster of little red votives, most of them long since melted to the ground. An elderly woman, her face stained with tears, snapping photos of the whole thing.

To know. The first, apparently easy definition is just this: to recognize, to identify, to be able to recall.

I brought Hannah to the shrine after school one day. She was eight at the time, and she felt she knew Junior, too. I wanted her, somehow, to remember him. Would she? She was three and a half when we moved to Oregon from Florida. Hannah and I met Junior almost right away, after our first Saturday farmers' market. We'd loaded up two bags with vegetables and berries and strolled over to a riverfront railing to look at the great Willamette. I didn't notice that there was a man behind us on a park bench. Didn't notice? No. Pretended to myself so thoroughly that I failed to see.

"They love cheese," said this voice. "Want to feed them some cheese?"

He came over and stood beside us, a dark-haired, weathered man in eyeglasses and a baseball cap, gesturing to the river.

"Sure," I said. I had to fight down a little fear. Was I taking a risk, talking to a stranger with Hannah there? What did I always tell her? Don't talk to strangers. The stranger was grinning at both of us. It was in his eyes, too: a big deep sense of humor. It shone out.

He had a couple of slices of American, each in its little cellophane envelope. He leaned on the railing, unwrapped one of them, and gave it to Hannah. "Go ahead, my friend," he told her. "Throw it in the river. They'll love you, they'll go crazy."

She did. The water boiled briefly, and quieted. She cried out with pleasure.

He gave her another.

After that, we saw him every time we went down there. Always in the same spot, always talking to somebody: a mother and her kids, a bunch of teenagers on skateboards. He had a shopping cart, but I never looked long enough to see how much—or how little—was in it. Later I found out that he called it his "chrome Cadillac" and was always pulling small treasures from it for people in need: a can of food, a warm shirt, a silver yin-yang necklace for a sixteen-year-old mother.

"Hello, you two, how've you been?" he'd holler. "You're lookin' good these days!" Usually I smiled or waved in response, but once I yelled back, "We're good. How've you been?"

"It's a beautiful day," he said. A little silence fell: only now, looking back, do I see that he didn't answer me. That a gap had been opened, and waited there.

We both closed it, I guess. He gave Hannah cheese to feed the fish, talked about the river, the good weather, told a couple of jokes. I didn't ask him anything more, and afterward I couldn't remember the jokes. Is that a failure too?

On the simplest level, *to know* is to pay attention.

In the winter, he took shelter under the post office eaves. We'd drive past, slipping letters into the box, but never get out of the car. Hannah saw him, though, from the backseat.

"Look," she said, the first time. "That's the man who gave us cheese to feed the fish."

Then I tried to tell her what I knew: that he had no place to live, that this was where he stayed in the winter. "It's too cold," she said. "Can we have him over sometime?"

"I wish we could," I said. "But we don't really know him—it might not be safe."

And on I drove, taking her with me back into the apparent safety of not knowing.

Standing at Junior's shrine that October day, Hannah observed everything with care. She got up close, read the notes on the torn scraps of paper, the lacy Hallmark cards, the typed-up messages tacked up beside his picture, some of them as long as letters.

"Stay as sweet as you are, June-Bug."

"You are missed, Junior."

"Take this as a lesson: If you live from paycheck to paycheck, you could wind up like this."

That fall, Hannah's Sunday school class was learning about mitzvahs. In Judaism, these are defined as good works, acts of true kindness, ethical deeds, little or big, private or public. Hannah brought home a mitzvah chart, and we taped it to the fridge, where she enthusiastically checked off a box each time she performed one. Here are a few: Washing your hands when you wake up in the morning. Thanking God for food. Helping a friend or sibling. Helping your parents. Praying to God. Inviting a friend to your house. Going to leave a candle at Junior's shrine. Could this be a mitzvah, however late?

The best mitzvah I can remember involved Junior. It happened the day I learned his nickname, and it happened, eerily, about a block away from the spot where he would be found beaten to death the next year, near the railroad tracks at Sixth and Western.

I'd stopped into the Dari Mart for some milk. Some laughter and talk near the cash register, and I turned from the glass dairy case to see. It was the fish-feeding man from the riverfront, with his baseball cap and glasses, the strange joy in his eyes. The clerk was handing him a jar of coins. This, it appeared, was a regular transaction. They weren't ushering him quickly out of the store, not calling the cops. No, they were helping him get by. There was banter, light flirting, an old, easy relationship between the two clerks and the man. Then the manager popped up from the back of the store. I held my breath: surely now it would happen, the inevitable warning, the reciting of rules and regulations, the shrugged apology. But no. The manager had in his hands a big flat pizza box. "Junior?" he said. "It's just plain cheese this time, no anchovies. You still want it? And watch out, man, it's really hot."

Junior, I thought, as I carried the milk to the car. Some people know him by name.

On the day of his death I learned his full name. His age. That he had family somewhere.

Enrique Elizario Sanchez, known as Junior. Forty-seven years old. "Authorities have contacted Junior's mother and sister, who live in New Mexico. No funeral services are scheduled."

The gap between those sentences is a canyon, an abyss, a place where stories drop soundlessly down and down. Where is the bottom? Does anybody know? Does God?

At the shrine we lit the candle we'd brought from home, a tall yellow prayer candle with a paper cover of Saint Joseph, protector of the earth. "It's so sad," said Hannah. "Look at all the flowers people brought; some of them look really expensive." A small crowd had gathered, a little river of grief not too far from the big one. "Goodbye, June-Bug," somebody whispered. "We'll miss you." It was almost Halloween, almost the Day of the Dead. Would the shrine last that long? A mitzvah—could all of us make it last till then? Beyond? Leaves skittered along the sidewalk; the air was cool and edged with late afternoon light, though the sidewalk had long since gone to shadow. But for a while no one walked away. Everyone had something to say, a story to tell about Enrique, Junior, June-Bug. If they didn't have one of their own, they told a story from the newspaper, or something they'd overheard here at the shrine earlier that day. Hannah herself began to speculate, to wonder how Junior had really died. She'd heard my story about the Dari Mart mitzvah, and now she said, "Maybe somebody was jealous of him, because people were so nice to him at the Dari Mart. Maybe somebody wanted what Junior had."

Maybe somebody wanted what Junior had.

Hannah was still reading the letters. "What does this mean?" she said, and I looked where she was pointing.

It said, "What if Jesus came back like this?"

She was crouched next to me, and I was trying to think of an answer, when a thin woman with a ravaged face and tears in her eyes stooped beside us and held out her own candle. "I forgot to bring matches," she said, biting her lip. "Can you light mine?"

"Sure," I said, and concentrated hard on the little flame, while my daughter waited for an answer.

Gardener's Journal

October 27

Kaisen: a lovely, warming soup to try. It's based on the one at the Japanese restaurant Koji in Portland, at Broadway and Alder, a small lozenge-shaped restaurant as snug and sweetly organized as a ship's galley. They've achieved some kind of fine balance there: I think the same people have worked there a long time, and have their choreography down and there is no false ambition. Just the desire to serve good food, and bring comfort.

Make a pork-bone stock. They get theirs at an Asian market in Portland; it comes in a big "milk-carton-like thing," the waitress told me. Put the pork bone, a quartered onion and some carrot into a pot of water (She didn't mention what spices!) Some slices of smashed ginger root, I'd think, and a few peppercorns. Cook for an hour, strain. Bring the broth back to a boil, and add fresh (and not too thin) ramen noodles and the following seafood: little strips of calamari steak, good-sized shrimp, and scallops. Cook briefly. Add lots of coarsely ground black pepper and finely chopped scallions.

October 28

Last Sunday, I drove to Garland Nursery with Kris. In a back room we found, on a shelf of discounted garden statuary, a tall stone bird bust (chicken head, I call it privately). It wears a little crown of some sort and has a marvelous smirk on its beak, with its eyes closed. With that smile, it has a Buddha-like calm and humor. "You have to get it for the Virgin shrine," said Kris, and then we saw the tag itself: "The Knight Gardener: someone has to fight the pests. With his night vision, his mission is to keep away evil critters, in the endless quest to grow organic."

Kris insisted on splitting the cost with me. She wouldn't let me go back home without it, and when we got to the house, she placed it in the shrine herself, angling it so that it appears to be gazing right into the kitchen window. We dragged T out of his study to see it. He laughed and said, "Well, that's good, we're safe now."

Kris's knee hurt when she bent to put the little god in his place. She winced hard. It's scary. Painful joints were among the first symptoms, last spring, of her lung cancer, which metastasized to her brain early this fall. But she's fearless: apparently the doctors told her it was *better* that it went into the brain than the bone marrow, if it was going to metastasize. And the tumor they took out, according to the surgeon, "was smaller than your fingernail, on the surface, and in a noneloquent part of the brain." The phrase made her laugh.

To everyone's amazement, she's started painting again. When they scooped out the little tumor, she asked the surgeon to take a photograph of it, and as startled as he was by the request, he'd obliged her. She's working now from these images. She's begun a diptych: one square contains an image of the tumor; the other, a deep red gloxinia. She'll take me to the studio to see it soon.

Later

After Kris went home to take a nap, I went back into the garden to sit for a moment in this strange stretch of fine clear days. No wind has come yet to rip the heck out of the trees, so they're still bright with leaves, like a New England fall, and it's been 70 degrees out. Everyone keeps saying, "Yeah, it's been great, but did you hear we're really going to get nailed this winter? Wetter and colder, they're saying."

What's going into the upper terrace? More of those irises from Kris's inexhaustible box (won't know their colors or varieties till spring). Two delphiniums (one Magic Fountain and one Pacific Giant in a deep intense blue), a yellow geum in the front corner, a four-foot-tall white phlox, and pale purple cranesbills here and there.

Kris, on the way home from Garland Nursery, had described a marvelous dinner party she and a friend put on during a trip to New York some time ago. A squid salad with vinaigrette and grapefruit slices (add the grapefruit late, as it gets mushy if you toss it too much); a striped bass poached in fish stock, served with a sauce of herb-garlic-anchovy paste that's mortar-and-pestled, then blended in a food processor with olive oil and egg to make an aioli. Serve with roasted rosemary potatoes, quartered garlic cloves, and carrots. "How would pearl onions go, too," Kris wondered aloud. "Too many elements?" We plan to try.

Are we really going to try to have a baby? We are forty-three and forty-five. But at a baby shower this morning, I couldn't let go of little Anna, six weeks old. I'd made up a box of Hannah's baby clothes for her, but couldn't give up the little sherbet-green newborn sweater that Naomi Shihab Nye bought me ten years ago in Niagara Falls from two old ladies on the Canadian side of the border. There's a whole story in that sweater, for the ladies chided her relentlessly about only having one child. I remember Naomi coming back to the writers' conference where we were teaching (we'd just met a few days before) with this lime-green sweater and a brown paper lunch bag full of fresh apricots from a farm stand. I was three months along and devoured the apricots, loved the green of the sweater. Now it has a tiny smudge of dirt on it from all its travels, and this was my excuse for not giving it away. I felt guilty for hoarding it, but somehow, it is more than a sweater, and I think it doesn't want to travel anymore. Lots of other nice things went into the box, however. After the party, as we walked out into the last bright October sunlight and leaves, T gave me the long steady look that wrecks me every time.

"Was that hard for you, seeing that baby?" he asked.

"You don't want to know," I joked.

"I *do* want to know," he said soberly.

So I admitted that, yes, the urge is still there, so powerful, so ridiculous. Then, after dinner, he asked me again. We talked some more, and even though it's scary for him, especially after the heart surgery—and we'd be old parents—he said, "Let's try and see what happens." We toasted each other with a glass of red wine.

October 29

The rains are here.

October 31

The rains *aren't* here yet. Not really. We've had two days of bright blue. The famous Halloween wind hasn't yet come to knock everything off the trees. Martha called yesterday, and we took a long hearty walk along the Bald Hill path. It's always good, rigorous exercise to keep up with her, and we talk absurdly fast, about everything: our kids, our work, our men—and, above all, our gardens. She's "had it up to here" (she made the swift, violent hand gesture at the neck) with the deer that rampage through her garden (she and her husband live in the hills above town). She's even tried spraying her peonies and roses with a blend of dish soap and jalapeño pepper juice. But this doesn't stop the deer. "One of these days," she said with a dark laugh, "you will find me in a cane rocker on my deck, leaning back in my gingham apron, shotgun raised. Wait and see."

T and I went back up Bald Hill today, at a somewhat slower pace. Everyone's out, everyone's stunned by the light, so golden it seems to be holding something off. The rains come with such regularity and vengeance here that we are tentative, can barely admit our pleasure. T says, "I will always remember this October," and I know he is talking about the way the darkness keeps holding off. Hannah, who adores the rain, explained to me why it rains so hard when it finally starts up in the late fall.

"Well, Mom," she says. "When it hasn't rained for so long—all summer—it *has* to rain hard. It's been holding its pee, and when it lets it go, there has to be a lot of it."

From Stephen Dunn's essay "Complaint, Complicity, Outrage and Composition":

> *To complain, protest, register outrage, are familiar impulses in most of our lives. . . . Yet Robert Frost wrote that "grievances are a form of impatience," and went on to say he didn't like them. . . . He preferred "griefs."*

November 1

Kris outdid herself for Halloween. Because her hair has grown back so wispily since the chemo, she's boldly shaved it, and for last night, she whitened her scalp into a "skull's head," blackening her ears and lips, and drawing teeth on her lips, outlining her eyes in black, and gluing on glittering gold fake eyelashes. Hands and feet in special black socks and gloves with bones raised on 'em. Black T-shirt with skeleton rib cage from the thrift store where she volunteers; it came to hand only today, she said, wide-eyed with pleasure. "Amazing, isn't it, the way that happens?" She danced with glittering ball lights tucked into her black sleeves. At one point at Squirrel's Tavern downtown, she was dancing with the Grim Reaper, and turned to me.

"Meet my friend Ed," she said, straight-faced, and I shook Death's hand.

She outlasted us all. T danced for a long time (red devil mask, which itched, so he wore it up on his head and looked like Little Bo Peep in a little soft bonnet) but got tired, and sat back down. At his request, I was Dead Carmen again this year: long black slip dress, hair up in a disheveled bun, red plastic rose between my teeth and red ribbon at the throat. This was my costume three Halloweens ago, a night we look back on to glimpse what we so studiously ignored at the time: that something not-quite-friendship was beginning to grow.

This time, on my way to the ladies' room in the crowded bar, a two-hundred-pound tooth fairy told me to shut my eyes and sprinkled me liberally with glitter. It was like being anointed, the way she smoothed it over my face.

We left a little after midnight. Later I heard that Kris closed down the bar. Alas, she didn't win the costume contest. The crown went to a very big Madeleine Albright in drag, but apparently Kris got plenty of applause as she paraded up and down the staircase. "I think I got People's Choice," she told us the next day.

The cowboy with the arrow through his eye had grasped her arm and said, "You got robbed."

This made her very happy.

November 3

At last, finished planting the whole box of irises Kris saved me, some in front, some in back, in front of Martha's honeysuckle-fence-to-be. No idea what they are, how tall, whether bearded or not, what colors. Iris anarchy.

Dreamed I was the singer Lucinda Williams and had a hit song climbing the charts. In the dream, I was visiting my mother in Southern California and said to her, "Mom, Mom, my song's on the radio; can we change the station from classical, just for a sec?"

"No way," she said. "Not on your life."

I called her up in the morning, told her the dream. She laughed. Then said, very firmly, "The dream is right. That kind of music drives me nuts. Of course I wouldn't let you change the station."

November 10

The garden is finished. All is withered. We had another stretch of stunning blue days, during which I did not go out and pull up the dead cosmos and whatever else needs pulling up: the last dahlia stems, the rapidly aging brown stalks of the cannas—oh, plenty. Now it's cold and overcast and I'm even less inclined to do it. Went out yesterday on my way to coffee with a former student and just yanked two cosmos stalks "in passing" in my good soft wool gloves, and was rewarded for my insouciance by good soft *wet* wool gloves. Must get serious.

November 12

Very dark outside. Surely the rains are imminent.

November 13

Hannah, for her Jewish studies class at our town's small synagogue, was asked to draw something on the subject of "the Garden of Eden." She got black construction paper and chalky pastels and produced this beautiful thing—a little cluster of bright leaves on a simple background, very pure. She said she got a big surprise when she accidentally colored some leaves more intensely (bright yellow-green, the veins outlined in thick black) and left another faint orange, with no interior color—she'd effectively backgrounded some leaves and foregrounded others.

"I think this is what Paul Klee does," she said.

I thought I'd faint. Later, she was tired and moody (waiting for a friend's birthday party later in the day) but at last got out her pastels and paper and sat on the couch with us and gave us a demonstration of how it worked.

I can die happy now.

November 14

The farmers' market has at last gone under the tin-roofed horse shelter at the fairgrounds. Each vendor has a sign that reads, IT'S NOT OVER TILL THE TURKEY GOBBLES. It's been pouring rain for a few days, and to get to the market stalls you must cross a rickety wooden plank laid across a small lake of mud. People wait politely on each side of the plank—"After you" . . . "No, no, after you"—everyone aware of the comedy of being there at all. Under the shelter, the vendors are bundled up, stamping feet, excessively friendly, for it is clear that the rain has hardened our customer-hearts. "Want a sample?" cries the apple lady, though I'm yards away. What is here? Apples, cider, filberts, squashes, honey. More apples. The very last of the tomatoes and peppers, these looking like they marched bravely up to the edge of ripe, then lost their nerve. The sweet Sun Gold cherry tomatoes of summer, which used to glow so hotly from their green cardboard pint boxes, are pale orange tinged with olive now.

The end is near, the fruits seem to cry. *Give it up or let it go.*

November 16

Two nights ago, T got down on bended knee in our neighborhood restaurant, Magenta, and asked me to marry him. I was laughing, trying to get my glasses off as he came at me. So happy it terrifies. We live on a brink all the time, even the most sheltered life. How is it that we are here together? Here at all?

After dinner, we went next door to a coffeehouse where a local band, the Tone Sharks, was improvising. The drummer sat on the floor with several plastic sticks, like a kid in preschool. But such fantastic sounds he made, even beating on the cheap carpet with plastic tubes! Sounded old, hollow, forested. They sat, reclined, flopped, these guys, and made their strange music. T, a rock 'n' roll drummer from deepest childhood, says the guy with the plastic sticks has an amazing left hand.

What I liked best about this scene was the elderly professor in his suit and tie, grading papers as the sax moaned, the trombone player moped, and the drummer worked himself into a climax. The old professor clearly knew them all: during the break he and the drummer had a quiet little chat. But best of all, when they commenced to play again, the gentleman took out a tissue, cleaned a pair of earplugs, and discreetly put them back in his ears.

November 19

Today's the twenty-third anniversary of Dad's death. Light yahrzeit lamp. Call Mom. Always such a weird day. A deep melancholy. A feeling that he's nearby, but can't make contact.

November 21

Woke up to brilliant blue skies. How can this be? Usually once the rains begin, that's it, *finis!* It's hard to settle down to work; light is flooding in through the lace curtains. Restless, I go downstairs and drink coffee, gaze out at the back garden, which soggily looks like it wants attention. There is nothing quite like the petulance of a neglected garden on a beautiful day in late November. What does it want from me? Is it time to hack off the sorry heads of the dahlias, pull the lemongrass out of the ground and put it a pot indoors, what, what, tell me! The dogwood has dropped all its red leaves, and they're beautiful there on the ground, like Hannah's picture of Eden. I don't want to disturb them. I'll wait.

Kris called. She has oysters to share, and good news: she got a clean bill of health from her oncologist in Portland. No new tumors, no nothing.

A good day to eat oysters.

Orfeo's Oyster

He loved the sea—does anyone know that about him anymore? It's music this and music that, the woodland animals coming his way, and children following in a dance, when the truth is, he dreamed only of water. Not just any water, either, but the kind between fresh and salt, and the first briny taste on the tongue. That was what gave him hope, for it was in such a place that he saw his bride go out, playfully waving, then disappear for good. It was in an estuary, with its deceptive calm, while blue herons lifted their heads, then gazed back down to something darting beneath—something he couldn't see—that he felt it most possible to begin his search. Here was a threshold: a place where one world might falter before the pull of another.

So it was that he floated on his back and let the water lift him. Musician that he was, he understood that a lift must necessarily lead to a fall. He lay on his back and waited, and as he did, the brine settled on his tongue and sang her own little melody to him, a melody of blue autumns, of ancient beds where a story so old nobody knew it anymore still played its melancholy song of waiting, of the hope for reunion and return.

So the brine seduced Orfeo, gathered him close just as the dark distance had once angled for Eurydice and taken her away. Eyes closed, he floated and listened. Was this song real? Was this the song that would help him bring her back? Maybe it was, because he swore he heard a strange, high keening. Then the world went greeny-black, and he seemed to sink.

They say he didn't recognize her at first. Her pink skin had gone a silvery-gray from being down there so long, and she wore a frilled and scalloped collar of black. She wore it like a slave, her head hung down, but all of her shining, nonetheless, in that watery light. Once she lifted her eyes, but they'd gone silver too, like polished candlesticks reflecting dim flames, from where he could not tell. But he also knew where he'd seen that light before. It had been in her blue-gray eyes the day they met, oh even on the day they wed. It was always there, and now he understood. Something had been waiting for her down here, just the way he waited up there.

He was told, and absolutely understood, the conditions of the deal. The rules, the required discipline, the likelihood of failure. Who can blame him for trying? He held on longer than any of us could have. But on the journey out, the mortal part of him began to rise, to hunger. He'd never felt more alone, more lost. Even the sound of her breathing disappeared, and all his cherished memories, one by one. But he was stubborn, and as he threaded his way through passages that wound and curled out of each other like dark arabesques, he heard a new music: one with corners and detours and drops where he thought there should be a rise. It refracted and dappled and the melody vanished for days at a time. He'd been a musician for a long time, and had some faith in the return of melody. He'd heard longer journeys than this on land. There on land—the melody always came back, eventually. But this was different. This was something else.

Is that what made him turn, just a little too soon? Was it the lure of a new music, a kind in which melody didn't have to come back? A music that his bride, for all her tenderness, must have known about and kept secret, a seed in her heart?

Or was it that other sound, the terrible keening that grew now, a chorus of all the dead, wanting to take advantage of an opening and rise along with her?

Everyone knows what happened next. How, leading her out, he couldn't resist a backward glance. And for a second, there she was: a candlestick of silvery-gray with her fading hint of flame. Her little ruffled collar of black. Then blackness, all.

And Orfeo stood, dripping and alone, cloaked in estuarine mud, his hands empty but his heart damp and full of weird new music, the color of herons, autumn, grief.

So the oyster waits in its shell, sometimes with a seed made against grit and desire, let in by the smallest breath. It's no accident that there is always music playing when you approach an oyster—if you dare approach at all. Nor is it accident that the oyster is not for everyone. It's a peculiar taste, a silken worry to the tongue, so tender it seems wrong.

But this won't stop you from hurting yourself, trying to pry one open at a party. And it's why, in the company of friends, you might feel suddenly alone—melancholy and ecstatic all at once. Take a moment. Notice that you hold in your hand a knife, and in your blood a startling, unreasonable urgency. And that when at last you put your tongue to the ruffled collar, you feel first a shudder of longing, and then an unaccountable desire to close your eyes.

Winter

Gardener's Journal

Without much gardening in it, I fear. Back on campus, back to teaching. Today a boy came to my office. He was in a writing class of mine, he said, a few years ago. I looked at him long and hard. I didn't recognize him: delicate features, skinny wrists, shirt and trousers bagging. A boy who lives on soup noodles. He leaned in the doorway and began to tell me about a writer I'd once recommended, James Alan McPherson, and how much McPherson means to him. I still couldn't remember this boy, but I believed him: I'm always recommending McPherson, and once again, he seems to have changed a life.

The boy's name is Aaron. "It's okay, you can come in, sit down," I said, and he edged carefully into the office, took a seat. I felt ridiculous, as if masquerading as the old, wise teacher. We talked for a half hour about books, and about where he has lived in the past few years: up to Portland, back down to Corvallis, trying to make a living so he can write. He told me that at the time he was reading McPherson's "Gold Coast," about an aspiring young black writer working as a janitor in a Cambridge apartment building, he himself was the janitor in a university physics building. The parallel consoled him, felt magical. Late at night, he'd put on headphones and listen to a book on tape of *Anna Karenina* as he scrubbed the long corridors. "It was a weirdly happy time," he said, and I remembered the sweet-scary depth of the world when you are young and living alone for the first time, accompanied—or so you think—only by art.

Just at that moment a current student thrust his head into the doorway. He did not, I know, mean to seem aggressive, but next to Aaron's near trembling, his sense of waiting for illumination with huge patience, this boy seemed an invader, coming to wrest from his teacher practical solutions, and perhaps a better grade imagined necessary for some future career. Aaron rose abruptly from his chair and looked at me—what was in that look? I felt like I knew it, remembered it from my own student days, both ecstatic and terrified; how I always lingered in my teacher's office door, fearing the emptiness, the uncertainty that waited just beyond. In her office I found the only reassurance that my desire to write had a deep taproot, any reality at all.

I looked at Aaron, a boy on the verge of revelation or the verge of annihilation—who could say? He would walk back to his little apartment, where, I hope, he has gathered to himself the talismans that give him faith. For at times he will no doubt think himself a fool or the greatest solipsist of all time. He will need all his books to revive the truth, and the first pure pleasure of the dream.

He'll need his *Anna Karenina* headphones and his beautiful, weird happiness.

"Come back anytime," I said, and meant it.

Will he? I don't know, but I'll never forget the image he gave me, of his own form gliding slowly down a long institutional hallway, Tolstoy's words in his ears and faintly, beyond them, the soft sound of the mophead brushing against linoleum. I see the ecstasy that burns in his face, the *Anna Karenina* look. How he looks as if literature really is enough to live on; literature, and soup noodles.

January 16

What would I say if I had to give a talk, *tomorrow*, on the writing process?

It might be interesting to take off from Stephen Dunn's discussion of the difference between grief and grievance in poetry.

The shadowy presence of a narrow perspective, of a secret anger and sense of victimhood, often wrecks a story and is the hardest thing for any of us to see in our own work and get past. It is devastating when a student comes to recognize it. It would be interesting to look at the way different story writers transform grievance into grief—or, to get more specific, the way they create an expansive, generous sense of characters for us, rather than pegging them, skewering them for quick ironic effect. Maybe start with the unreliable narrator of Margaret Atwood's "Rape Fantasies," whose office gal complains in one long tirade, right up to the last second, when the curtain parts and we glimpse the secret grief she's been concealing all along. Grievance into grief, just like that. Could she have gotten there without the extremity of the "whine"? And there's Alice Munro's "Material," which begins as an *apparently* one-note rant that is, in fact, stippled from the get-go with little ledges and drop-offs suggesting a countercurrent, a more complex view of the ex-husband and herself.

I'd want to wind up with Welty, the master of the generous treatment of character, somehow balancing irony and compassion. I'd go with *The Golden Apples* and Miss Eckhart, the comical old-maid piano teacher who finally emerges as a figure of tremendous depth, a woman who, playing the "wrong music" during a great thunderstorm, briefly reveals her own talent to her young pupils, so that they see the violent power of art. Welty had to expand her point of view to a lyrical omniscience to get there. A line in one of her essays in *The Eye of the Story* says it all. The writer's job, she tells us, is "not to point the finger in judgment but to part a curtain, that invisible shadow that falls between people, the veil of indifference to each other's presence, each other's wonder, each other's human plight."

January 19

Got a letter from one of my former Florida undergraduates; she'd read an essay of mine about Florida and said, among other things, that it freaked her out to see that I, her teacher, had had a life of my own while she'd been taking my class. T and I laughed over this—a little nervously, partly because there are days, even whole weeks when the quiet little space of the writing life shrinks almost to nothing against the *social* immediacy of teaching. But there's another fear beneath that. The truth is, we exist for our students primarily in our roles as functionaries to *their* work, their dreams. Oh, of course they want us to have reputations as writers, but even this is only so they can claim us as part of their own narrative of development someday. It's hard not to disappear into that role. Nor do I blame them; I'm sure I did it myself.

Phil Levine has a great story about the poet John Berryman as a teacher at the Iowa Writers' Workshop. All the students enrolled in Robert Lowell's class, because Lowell was already famous. The "overflow" students shuffled into Berryman's, feeling rejected and second best. But it turns out he was the great teacher, the dark horse. Sure, later he'd be a legend of poetry too, and his famous students, such as Phil Levine, could write stories about their once-not-famous teacher. But that's not what gets to me. It's Berryman *then*, throwing himself so fully into the work of teaching, holding nothing back, giving to his students like there's no tomorrow.

Whether it's a known or an unknown writer who teaches, the thing to aspire to is the single potent gesture, a sentence of writerly advice enough to live on, to sustain for life a young *possible* writer. Oh, to do that.

The Butterfly on the Blackboard

She was twenty-eight, a PhD student in American literature at the University of California, Davis, assigned to teach composition to freshmen. At the time I was eighteen and had not considered how grim a job this might be, how the students might look back at a graduate teaching assistant with apathy and outright disdain. And as we walked in, she was drawing a butterfly on the blackboard, from which, that hour, a metaphor of composition would somehow emerge. It's been decades, and I can't remember the details of the analogy, only the butterfly itself, her hand shaping it swiftly, and the brevity of her explanation, the way it left a kind of opening in me, as if between the image of the butterfly and her words there lay a shadow shape of my own, a possibility beginning to form.

It was fall term, 1975. The class met at eight in the morning, and I think now that I was in love several different ways: with the deepening weather of October in Northern California, with the dark blue sweater I wore nearly every day, with E. B. White's "Once More to the Lake" and James Agee's *A Death in the Family*—and, now I know, with my teacher, too. When I reread certain writers—Woolf, Agee, White, Welty—I smell autumn and hear her voice: a little like fall itself, husky and shy, but with a final crisp certainty at the ends of words, as if she'd been trained as a singer. A diva's confidence, without a diva's attitude—is that possible?

She rarely spoke about herself. Still, we all sensed some buried talent she had deliberately laid aside but retained within her, a ghostly twin.

Then one day, unexpectedly, she told us a story that should have explained it, that began to explain it, but finally didn't. Something remained unsaid, haunting us like a painting or the best, most elusive short story.

The episode took place when she was eighteen, which I think now was why she told it—most of us were at this age, fragile, self-consumed, and deeply unaware. It was a tale of youthful ambition, a failure that might have ended in death—and nearly did. It seems she'd won a national photography competition, and been given, as the prize, a plum assignment: to photograph, for *Life* magazine, a day in the life of Wales. Off she went, full of fantasies and bravado, with a new camera, a car and an expense account, a fine winter coat. What happened next she could not or would not say, only that as the Welsh winter set in, she began to falter. By January she'd sold the camera, the car even the coat. One day she wound up shivering and hunched over in abdominal pain, on the stoop of a village house, while a housewife in an apron swept carefully around her. How she was rescued—by self or other—she must have told us, though all I remember is that she nearly died, and I sensed, though I do not believe she said this, that she would never fully recover her health. But she was rescued, hospitalized, saved. And though she gave up the assignment, she stayed on, in a cottage in Devon, where, she told us, she still had very dear friends.

Yet neither the rescue nor the failed assignment was the haunting thing: it was the bleak moment on the stoop, how easy it was to fall, how fast you could go, that you could, in spite of every advantage, be swept out with the morning dust and garbage. I remember thinking, a little desperately, *How is it you're alive, and here to tell us this story?* In the class, we were reading George Orwell's *Down and Out in Paris and London*, and I see now that she was implicitly—and perhaps deliberately—linking a published famous piece of literature by a great dead man to her own personal, oral—and full of holes—account of a person standing before us in an unprepossessing way, in a beige sweater and tweed skirt. To be honest, it is her story, and not Orwell's, I remember best, but more significantly, she gave me the lifelong habit of calling up both literature and personal stories in times of trouble and need, without regard for literary hierarchy.

It wasn't long after—maybe just two years—that I came to need her story, and Orwell's, and came to understand the crucial thing about them both: the warning that we can fall, with very little effort indeed, and that in fact we have it in us to *will* that fall, a disappearance unto death.

I had taken my junior year abroad, in Scotland, and while I was there, my father, ill with acute leukemia, died of complications from chemotherapy. I went home to Southern California for his funeral, then returned to Scotland, grief bottled up in me under other names: guilt, loneliness, self-absorption. At the end of a winter flu, I found myself lying on my bed in my rented room, contentedly considering suicide. It seemed much easier than anyone had suggested: all you had to do was to stop eating, and lie there until you faded, vanished into thin air. When I hear myself say this now, I think immediately of Kafka's Gregor Samsa in "The Metamorphosis," who leaves his bug body behind, an empty husk, but whose spiritual presence we feel spreading like the early spring light over the end of the story and all his family as they move ahead into new life.

Of course I thought no such thing at the time. I wasn't interested in stories of sacrifice and redemption, but absorbed myself in the furious, passionate, adolescent unhappiness of early Dostoyevsky, poverty and inexplicable fevers and yellow oilcloth and clerks with rotted teeth, eager to erase your name. Lying on my bed, I shrugged and thought, *How ugly those chimneys and rooftops are, how sordid!* and closed my eyes against life.

I was lucky: there came, within a day or two, a knock on the door: some of my classmates and our program director, on their way to supper in town, had "dropped by" to see if I wanted to join in. They were all very casual, but I felt my condition all the more acutely—how *different* I was from all of them, pure Gregor Samsa, pure *bug*. I couldn't seem to say or do anything normal. Long after, I discovered the obvious: that the director had been alerted to my absence from classes and had arranged an intervention of sorts. But at the time, it seemed simply an accident that they should all be standing in my room, inviting me along for supper. At that meal, the director sat beside me, chatting kindly and easily about bicycle trips and whatnot, while I pushed my food around on my plate. Then, without warning, and so quietly I nearly missed it, he said, "There will be dark days. You can't expect them not to come." He looked at me, and as if he'd touched a spring, I wept. Wept and began the slow process of coming back to the world.

At the end of the evening he wrapped up my uneaten supper and walked me home. I think I threw out that steak, but I ate, the next day, a very fine soft-boiled egg on toast, and did an errand for my landlady, who, it turned out, had also made a call to the director. I was lucky: rescued by community, the cycle broken. Only then did I remember my teacher's story, realize she'd been around this age, and alone in a foreign country, when she'd had her breakdown. That she must have laid herself on someone's stoop to save her own life.

The gift of her story—the only personal one she ever told— seems to be its unfinished or unexplained quality. She left it open, not just to interpretation, but to future use. It belonged to all of us, the way Dostoyevsky does, and Kafka and Orwell, and I imagine that at least a few other students in the class carried it forward into the next fragile years of growing up, like a secret envelope in the valise, to be opened and recognized only on the point of necessity, when we need to know that we are not alone. Surely the story meant different things to all of us, at different times, but was always recalled, I imagine, when we saw how terribly alone the human being is in pain, shivering on whatever stoop, in danger of vanishment before we are ready.

I think my teacher endured her students' fragility and appalling eagerness because it was her vocation to do so: to cultivate shapely, honest prose wherever she could, in the most ragged and vulnerable gardens, in deserts and bogs, wherever. I think I would fall into the category of bog: everything I wrote was soggy with adjective and simile; I imagine her now digging between the heavy clumps of unnecessary plantings for some small, straight truth. I once handed her five drafts of a four-page essay and said brightly, "Tell me which one is best!" She read them while I sat there—God knows it probably didn't take long to make that diagnosis—and handed them all back at once.

"You can do better than this," she said. "Just tell me what happened."

I wept. I was always weeping then, and maybe many of us were, because she had a box of tissues handy in her desk drawer, on the student-chair side. While I blew my nose, she gave further instruction. Go out for pizza, she said, and play a couple of games of pinball. Before you go to bed, set your alarm for six, sharpen several pencils, and lay these, with a notepad, on your nightstand. Then, in the morning, start writing without thinking at all. Just tell me what happened.

When I came out of the English Studies building that evening, another student from our class was leaning against the wall, smoking a cigarette. He was the only adult in our class—a psychology major, returning to school after dropping out years before. He was twenty-eight, the same age as our teacher, he told me ruefully. Like our teacher, he had about him a difference: a dignity and a hidden burden. It seemed to give him a calm I envied, feeling as I did that my own core was a fragile little stem of green, always in danger of wilting. At any rate, I felt a sort of comfort in his presence, a trust. He was dark-haired, with weary, gentle eyes; he loved her class too. I suppose the whole story was in my face, because he asked me if I'd had dinner yet, gravely, sweetly. It was almost romantic, in the perfect "almost" way: neither of us, I think, had any interest in tipping it. I don't recall that we spoke of anything but writing and books that night—though we did play two games of Pac-Man, watching the little yellow round creatures devour each other. I made my way home with the magical feeling that his presence outside the English building had been fated: not so much a sign that I was on the right path, but that my teacher's way was the right one, that I should carefully follow it.

I sharpened the pencils, laid out the paper, set the alarm, and in the morning, with a feeling of disgust and dread and rapidly failing nerve, wrote something down. Naked, flat prose. Not a single metaphor or simile. Nothing but the facts, ma'am. I hated it, and felt as though I would never write again, stripped as I'd been of all illusion, nothing to do but the job of telling it. What's that line from Flannery O'Connor, when the Misfit says, "Shut up, Bobby Lee. It's no real pleasure in life"? I felt I'd murdered my story, destroyed its passion, and turned it in "as is," with a sense of disgust, on notepaper, in scrappy pencil.

Two days later it reappeared, neatly typed, with copies handed out to everyone in the class, my own marked with a grade so high I began to perspire lightly in my seat. She had changed my name to Katherine (which I liked; it was dignified) and read it aloud to the class. It feels childish, bragging, to repeat this story now, but in that moment, I understood that I had been taught, and had learned, something about the art of writing. I sat in my little pool of sweat and experienced a bliss that I knew had no relationship to my wretched effort, and knew, absolutely, that I would have to return to the wretched effort again and again. The bliss of acceptance was neither substitute nor even, finally, reward. It was separate, unreal, a thing to get past as quickly as possible, for bliss could derail you for life. I think now she was putting me through a whole process, from rejection to wholesale revision to the illusion of reward. She wanted me to have the whole thing: the real life of writing, head down, scratching out whatever you had, without illusions, in the dark of early morning.

She took it a step further: taught me how to "send out" and gave me my first taste of rejection out there. "Thank you," wrote an editor at *Seventeen*. "Unfortunately, this has too much death in it for us. But do try your hand at something else!"

The last piece of advice my teacher gave me was the most haunting, and came, again, after I thought I'd done my best for her.

"Someday," she said, "you'll learn to tell the truth."

I saw her off and on during my time at UC Davis. Once, she invited me over for lunch—this, too, feels in hindsight like a mystery, though at the time, it was only the glamour of it, the prestige, that I felt: true, final acceptance at last! I remember her place as a cottage, though in fact it was a modern one-bedroom apartment that she had transformed into a home of such comfortable clarity and privacy that I remember it so: in my eyes it was a small, exquisitely snug country dwelling. She was, at the time, living alone, though she alluded once, with her characteristic brevity, to a recent relationship, *over now*. I listened hard, but could detect no bitterness or grief. There it was again: a central piece of a story she wouldn't reveal, an emotion undisclosed, which seemed to point toward a larger tragedy deeply hidden. It was this I was drawn to, wanted to learn from, drink from, and seems related now in my mind to Eudora Welty's comment that "if . . . fiction [seems] full of mystery, I think it's fuller than I know how to say. Plot, characters, setting and so forth, are not what I'm referring to now. . . . [T]he mystery lies in the use of language to express human life."

My teacher was, I think, my personal Welty, until I got to know that writer's work and felt I could cling to it, a lifeboat of fiction. Like Welty, my teacher was modest to the point of self-sacrifice, and deeply marked by the way she experienced life. And so it felt like the greatest privilege to be let into her house: to come at all near the life behind the life anyone allows you to see. The rose-and-white china she served lunch on had belonged to her grandmother, and she made a beautiful simple lunch of salad and soup, with tea afterward, and I wanted to absorb the moment, to imitate it later. The care and simplicity of her things, her way of respecting her private world, I still yearn to feel myself. I aspire; it eludes me. Not long ago I came across this passage by M.F.K. Fisher, and though my teacher's house was nothing so exotic, I was reminded instantly of it, of its personality, purely hers, and realized, late, that I'd been inside the refuge of a solitary.

> Sue lived in a little weather-beaten house on a big weather-beaten cliff. At first when you entered it, the house seemed almost empty, but soon you realized that . . . it was stuffed with a thousand relics . . . lump-filled cushions that Whistler had sat on, and a Phyfe chair that had one stormy night been kicked into kindling wood by Oscar Wilde. . . . [Y]ou ate by one candle . . . everything from one large Spode soup plate. . . . I have never eaten such strange things as there in her dark smelly room, with the waves roaring at the foot of the cliff. . . . She put them together with thought and

gratitude, and never seemed to realize that her cuisine was one of intense romantic strangeness to everyone but herself.

After lunch, my teacher cleared the plates and led me to the door and said good-bye, and I felt the same thing I'd felt on the first day of class, that one door had been closed and another, somewhere else, opened. Once again she was offering me a partial story and the right moment for departure. Because finally, this is the only gift the writing teacher can give. John Berger says that "without mystery, without curiosity and without the form imposed by a partial answer, there can be no stories—only confessions, communiqués, memories and fragments of autobiographical fantasy."

We never deny that there is mystery in good writing—in both the process and the result—but we rarely hear talk of the mystery of good teaching. The profession falls more and more into the hands of those who would try to quantify it, to be constantly tested and poked until it spits back a technical reply. But we would do well to acknowledge the unquantifiable, untraceable moves of our most gifted teachers—and I do not mean famous or even necessarily charismatic, but *gifted* in the way of a musician or writer or painter, or anyone who opens us up to the surprise of the new, the never-before-known. For though it happens in teaching as it does in these other arts, it happens, for some reason, without our notice. Maybe this is necessary. Maybe great teaching does its work best in the cracks and obscure places, only to be discovered long after it has accomplished its alchemy in yet another student.

That lunch wasn't the last time I saw my teacher, but it feels like it. The story between us, a mystery in itself, ended that day at her apartment door. I knew, undeniably, that she was withdrawing her attention—her wisdom and sanctuary—from me. Necessarily, intelligently. It was time for me to set out on my own. We corresponded once or twice after she got her first teaching job back East, but there came a day when she did not answer a letter. I tried once more, and got no reply.

I felt, of course, rejected, and cast about in my mind for ways I might have irritated her. I cannot honestly say that I've gotten over it—maybe it was, in fact, a form of first love, and there is, thank God, no getting over that.

Recently, a former student of mine sent me a batch of poems and a letter recalling our work together. It was unusual: not a letter asking for recommendations or specific help of any kind. And it was written with considerably more dignity than my own to my teacher had been, though with that same youthful enthusiasm to show the teacher what has happened *since*. It has been some months now, and my student's letter, and her very fine poems, are still on my desk. I am glad she wrote to me, and I keep meaning to reply when I have a little time. Every once in a while I look at her letter and the poems, and then at the swamp of immediate teaching tasks, and want to do none of them but go to the "other" desk, the one where my novel waits, itself abandoned.

What does this silence mean to my student? Will a painful fiction of abandonment shape itself, a suspicion of having displeased? Or will she, more healthily, be angry and feel that I've failed her—how hard could it be to make a reply? She may, as I once did, send a second letter, hoping to "win back" some lost relationship.

But time will pass, and gradually the anxiety will fade. Other attachments will arise to replace this one. Then one day, at forty-three, she will be standing in her garden and receive just such a letter from a student of hers, and be glad, then set it aside, intending to reply a little later, and go back to her desk, to her work, which waits hungrily now, forever on the verge of abandonment. She will dig in, a student once more, intent on her own struggles and nobody else's, and one day she'll discover that she never wrote back. She'll think briefly, guiltily, of her student, and then, just maybe, of her old teacher—surely an old woman by now! Only then will she understand the necessity of silence, and remember for both of us the butterfly on the blackboard, the teacher's hand only a shadow now, a gesture made long ago, on our behalf, between the teacher's mystery and our own.

Gardener's Journal

What is it about winter and this journal? Ages seem to have gone by. Of course we are madly busy with teaching, travel, Hannah . . . but why this silence? Is it the dormant time? Linked to the season, and the garden? It was briefly sunny and warmer this morning, and I found myself out in the back garden, frowning at rampant small weeds and the mucky leaves I spread over plants a month ago when a big freeze was predicted. (The freeze didn't—but still could—materialize.) I attacked some of the little guys, felt the pleasure of being out there, bent over the wet, wet earth, but also felt overwhelmed by how much there is to do, even in the smallest of gardens. And my imagination falters, still. It's winter, of course, a cruel time to judge, but the ground covers, some of them, have gone brown or yellow in the center, and under the blue spruce, they're nearly buried in needles. I'm thinking that right under the spruce, and perhaps in other places too, ground cover isn't the answer. Maybe ferns and other shade plants, to create more height and structural interest, more mass and small architecture beneath. In spring, I'll have a better idea. Right now, I should just attend to the weeds. And note: the purple crocuses are coming up! That will be lovely to see. All sorts of surprises, since I planted them randomly. It's hard to imagine what it's going to feel like when they start the demolition and construction next door. Chris, the chief architect on the Newman Commons project, used that word today for the first time—demolition.

Later

Forgot to say that T bought me a 35mm camera and we went out a couple weeks ago and took a roll of black-and-white around the Newman Center property. Particularly fine is T's picture of one of the little angled windows that jut out from Hillside with their flared hoods. The place looks slightly enchanted, the way neglected, vulnerable buildings do. I need to take pictures inside, too, before it comes down. The infrequent meetings with the architect and design landscapers are disconcerting, though I'm impressed by their expertise, how they have to work within the restrictions of a commercial site. The landscape guy says, "I can't go dropping posies everywhere," by which he means he can't plant perennials, has to stick to "serviceable" easy-maintenance ground covers and shrubs. I'm constantly asking for odd things, not knowing what I'm talking about. Can you plant shrubs that look like perennial flowers, not boring institutional stuff? God, they must hate working with neighbors! I mean to go look at David D.'s own garden—he's the local planning consultant representing the Portland developers and lives, himself, in a 1929 bungalow on a very busy street downtown. He's created what looks, at a quick glance, like a Chinese classical garden. He says he's got some weird varieties of tropical fruit trees in there that will survive our winters. I want a tour. It's his eye that may ultimately shape our surrounding landscape.

February 4

Hannah talked tonight about being afraid of her body, about the way it's going to change as she grows up. She's afraid that when she has breasts, she won't be able to do kid things, like jump on a trampoline, and that they'll hurt when people bang into them. And she's got a new hyper-alertness, too: she says she notices how she's swallowing, and then is afraid she'll forget *how to*. Or she gets in a pattern of "blinking," as if with every blink she is taking a picture of someone. She says—this at first frightened me—that voices tell her to do these things, the blinking and so on, and that they "annoy" her. This is something to keep an eye (or ear) on, though it sounds very familiar, and when pressed, she says they're not really voices, exactly. And it only seems to happen when she's unoccupied. I remember something like this in childhood—for instance, repeating a word (*world* is the one I remember) until it had no meaning anymore, and even the letters looked foreign, meaningless. I felt crazy, but couldn't stop myself. Is this natural? An awakening to a consciousness of the body? She just turned ten in January. Where did I read that around nine or ten a child first awakens to the reality of death? How amazing, to see a girl go through this, her fear of the unknown, of not knowing what's next. She already dresses like a preteen, in jeans and long-sleeved T-shirts, a dark olive-green sweater, very demure and understated in her tastes, and has this compact, slim body. At school she is teased for being small but claims it doesn't bother her. Wants, suddenly, to go to France. Is it because I read to her from Colette's "The Long-cat"? Nothing else will do!

February 7

It rained in the night, and when Hannah and I came out to the car this morning, she said, "Stop, take a big whiff." I breathed in, and she did too, again, and said, "I love that smell." How lovely, her wanting to stop and take a big whiff; already the urge to stop the onward rush of life—I am verging on cliché, aren't I, but damn, it was marvelous to see her conscious of the weather. Come to think of it, she also made me look up while I was digging for my keys, and there they were, dusky Canada geese flying in formation. "Which direction is that?" she wanted to know. "Southwest," I said, and she grinned. "Thank God, they're on their way," she said, and I remembered that earlier this month she'd said she was worried they wouldn't migrate at the right time. I explained that they were not really leaving; we always think they're flying south as spring gets near, but the fact is that they *winter* in the Willamette Valley and head north to Alaska in the spring. As I write this, I can hear more of them honking overhead, quite close.

Took Hannah to school, came back, and had the urge to garden. It is of course winter, and there is nothing sensible about this urge. But it goes along with the renewed "staring" into the backyard, and my sense, every time I pull into the driveway, that there's a kind of slimy mush in the front terraces, not to mention that nasty blackberry vine that bugged me all summer, snagging me as I reached in for other things. Its roots have been exposed by winter starkness. I didn't see them, actually, until I cut back everything else in the vicinity: the lithodora and lavatera and that tall graceful verbena that Martha says is called "a see-through or scrim plant" because it's like a transparent theater curtain you can see behind. Still I had to pull that curtain aside to bring the hidden naked nasty vine to light for all to see— or, rather, for me to dig out. I took it on with proper theatrical aggression. Put on a heavy sweatshirt and gloves and went forth with shovel and the small simmering outrage I bear toward it, dormant for months.

I got it out, not without pain. Blackberry is a vine that does not like to be interfered with. But the upshot was that once I got out there, I discovered that the air was downright balmy—nearly 60 degrees, I'm guessing, and the birds were busy after seeds, very noisy, and it was damn pleasant out on the street, with everyone walking to and from campus. So I got my shears and clippers and trowel and worked for another hour, giving the Siberian iris, the coreopsis, and the penstemon their wildly overdue winter haircuts, pulling away the slimy gunk of the summer's calla lilies, and generally tidying up. Gradually the elegiac mood settled on me, a sort of sweet melancholy awareness of time passing, not in an anxious, I-can't-get-it-all-done way, but awareness of this moment, with its village-urban noises of Monroe Street, trucks, bikes, walkers, and the manic birds in the dryer vents of the apartment building across the street. All of it seemed very gentle and sad and going fast. The Newman Commons project will change the light, and its height, its clock tower and cross, will loom here. Next year at this time I'll be gardening in the shadow of construction, and it will feel different. It might be interesting, the high contrast of big machinery against little trowel, and while

I wish, wish, wish it weren't coming, that we could keep our little piece of human-sized landscape from getting crowded out by the institutional, I'm trying to stay curious—to hell with objectivity, but curious—asking questions, watching for the minute changes rather than the gross, obvious ones.

For some time I've been meaning to write about Ilya Kabakov's *School No. 6*, housed in an old army barracks on the outskirts of Marfa, Texas, where the Chinati Foundation has its exhibits. T and I visited the place in December. Kabakov has re-created an abandoned Soviet schoolhouse. It's an art "environment," an installation. There were about ten of us on the tour: a small group of well-heeled citizens from Dallas, a hip young couple, and three very young men, college students I'd guessed, from Japan.

The first room is purely the schoolroom: a few desks haphazardly strewn about, tattered posters falling off the walls, and on the floor, a scattering of broken pencils, dolls, old postcards, and advertisements torn out of magazines. You nearly hear their voices, though there is no sound—so smart not to *have* sound; you create it in your head. Walls mint green below, dirty white above, peeling even! The guide tells us that originally Kabakov wanted all the windows left open or broken, as well as the doors, so that the elements would weather the exhibit naturally, but apparently nature is a little too aggressive in Marfa; in the end they had to board up the windows, but left the courtyard doors open. Hence the very odd thing that happened. In the second and third rooms, there were glass cases with "artifacts" and descriptions in them—a wadded-up piece of paper with the caption, "This is the note Sofia wrote to Ivan on Tuesday" and another saying, "This is the spitwad that started the fight between the boys." You get the idea. Artifacts of a child's life, what is significant, memorable. On one of these glass cases, a grasshopper was precariously poised. I stared and stared; was it part of the exhibit or real? I couldn't walk away from that grasshopper until I knew, but I also didn't want to break it by accident if, in fact, it was made of glass or ceramic or whatnot. Finally I found a twig on the floor (was it, too, part of the installation?) and touched the grasshopper's foreleg lightly. It twitched and snapped away.

"Ah, real," I said, and turned to see the three boys from Japan watching me with great curiosity. I had, myself, become part of the exhibit.

February 20

The journal has gone dormant yet again, hibernating with the garden. This is my first day back at my desk in ages. I let the university job whisk me away, and the price—if I can describe it—is a feeling of having allowed myself to shrink at the core, old apple core, the place I write from, gone back down to compost, but that's too pleasant a way of putting it. I can hear in it my wishful thinking that this is a wholesome and useful absence, one that will lead to renewal. It is never useful to stop writing. The fact is, I have been lazy, have let *all* the layers of life, the consequential and the apparently not, take hold of me, own me. Here and there, a little burst of language, a brief glimmer of dreaminess would try to rise, but I shoved it down brutally, I was untender to it. But here are some things to come back to, as I push the little rotted spot open and air it out like a stinky neglected room (say, Gregor's in "The Metamorphosis," which my undergraduates recently got passionate about, how astonishing!). First of all, our brief trip to Boston in late January, part business, part pleasure, and Hannah's magical feeling about the view out my friend's daughter's bedroom window, the snowy yards and orange streetlamps of Watertown, the way the hill dropped away, the red radio tower lights in the distance. "Is that New York City?" she asked. Then there was her pleasure at discovering the whimsical artwork of Edward Gorey, at the café called Curious Liquids on the corner of the Commons by the State House; what extreme pleasure she took in his spidery, black-cloaked Victorians. Then, the next day in a bookstore with T in Cambridge, I found Rilke's *Letters on Cézanne*, with its breathtaking passages about color and the "thingness," the "hard reality" of Cezanne's painting, which reminds me of what Alice

Munro does in her stories, the way she is constantly trying to get at the hard knuckle of reality, with no covering, no illusion, though of course when you're writing it's all illusion. But her style proceeds by building, then refuting storyness, the sentimental, the lies we tell ourselves and others for every conceivable reason; she ravels it out, then strips it ruthlessly away, then lets it build again.

I've been teaching her stories lately to a small graduate class, and it's been a joy. One young woman in particular has shown a muscular toughness and pleasure in debate, refutation, definite opinion. She is metamorphosing, she has real strength in her, and real talent; I hope she prevails. I enjoy her frowning, slightly irked look when we disagree, the depth of her seriousness about literature, so rare. And as a real student should, she's smacking up against my stubbornness, and I feel it for the first time, my deep stubbornness. What a luxury, in the classroom, to feel that boniness, to become conscious of it. I have become more aware of my weaknesses and flaws as a person, but in an interesting, not entirely upsetting way. Sometimes I just plain old see it: a moment when I've been ungenerous, narrow-hearted, stubbornly locked into a view. But lately seeing myself thus doesn't fill me with the old dread and embarrassment. I just think, *Oh, you could have done that better; that was low.* What is it in Jane Austen's *Emma* that the brotherly lover says? "Badly done!" I must play that role myself now—no one is instructing me. T never has and never would; it doesn't seem to exist in him as a possibility, that "judging" impulse. His *not judging* makes me want to stand up and see myself without defensiveness. To say, Yes, I am stippled with weak bits, stippled and flecked, like a paintable surface with innate flaws. Can't ever clean that stuff off, will have to paint on it, layered as it is. How new, that feeling.

Last evening, as dusk fell, T and I listened to a tape recording of Larry Levis's poem "The Perfection of Solitude: A Sequence." The tape was made last summer at Warren Wilson College, where T was teaching writing—right around the time he started feeling the pressure and pain in his chest. He and some other faculty members read the poem out loud. At first I couldn't fully concentrate, seduced by the beauty of T's voice, so familiarly tender and so nearly lost to me—all that quiet fierce meticulous drive. I can't seem to get past that feeling, fear and gratitude all mixed up. Anyway, the poem begins with images of an Oaxacan plaza held still by the observer in memory:

> This moment, not one leaf is moving, & the cloud bank above it all
> Does not move . . .
> . . . I remember gazing at the plaza the whole time so that
> Nothing would change, so that nothing would ever change. . . . Five seconds
>
> Later a bomb went off in the telegraph office & a young janitor who was
>
> Sweeping up the place felt both his legs surprise him with their sudden
> Absence.

There it was again: this battle between the urge to hold time still by making art and the instant violence and chaos of the world rushing in to crush the illusion. The "bomb" of chaos is out in the world, but also inside our hearts. The snow globe held so carefully in the hands can shatter in an instant, the whole delicate architecture splintered and gone. Ribs and lungs and spine, windows, voice.

Is this the tension that lives beneath even the desire to shape a small domestic sanctuary? Is everything we do a way of evading the terror of chaos, of loneliness, of the loss of the illusion of control over our fragile lives? Levis doesn't just face this reminder of death: he *woos* it. He talks about saying a name over and over again until it detaches from the person and regains its freedom from our making impulse.

I'm reminded of Hannah's fear of forgetting how to swallow, and of my own childhood repetition of the word *world* until it lost its meaning. It starts to take me back to that moment in Scotland, where I lay on a bed and thought I could stop eating, and relinquish my life, my beating heart, just like that. How remarkable, though, to feel such a thing and write through it. Hold it in your hand as you would the snow globe. Just hold it.

Levis died at forty-nine of a heart attack. I can't help but think of this, as I listen to T read the poem. It seems a miracle all over again, that he's here with me: a living voice in the rooms of our house, eyes blue-green again, cheekbones underlain with light.

February 23

Last night at dinner, I was telling T about Natalia Ginzburg's notion of being "the recording angel" of her family. T says that somewhere he ran across a similar quote from Nadine Gordimer: that one should write as if one were already dead. Anna Akhmatova also has this quality, he says. It's what he fell in love with when he read her, in his twenties—like M.F.K. Fisher, she had terrible tragedy in her life, but wrote about it with deep sensuality, courage, and forgiveness, of herself and others.

This is what Levis does, too. Fisher, it seems to me, offers a more tender, buoyant version. More possible, somehow, for me to reach for.

February 25

Attended a meeting at the Newman Center with a man we've never met before: a priest who is also a lawyer and real estate developer, somehow. This is Father Matt, from the Catholic Archdiocese of Portland, which, it turns out, is the entity behind the proposed development, not really the local Newman Center. It's a bit daunting. The legal team is from Portland, too, and so are the architects. A dozen neighborhood folks showed up, as well as the architects and land-use planners. In the air, the whole time, was a not-so-implicit threat: they said they were offering us "the lesser of two evils." Would you rather have a Pizza Hut here? Father Matt asked us. Or, even worse, a *commercial* developer? It is perhaps debatable that their "nonprofit corporation" is any different than a commercial developer. They are soliciting our input on color and landscaping, but we are still looking at four stories and sixty-four student apartments, and the loss of many trees, including our beloved elm. Did I say "our" elm? Funny, though it's not on our property, it is the first thing I see when I open my eyes each morning, through the skylight. Chris, the chief architect, doubts it can be saved. Their arborist has told them that "elms are subject to disease, especially one this old," as if this is a further reason to cut it down.

Anyway, it was a tough meeting. Our friends Trish and Kent, former city council members, asked great questions, but to no avail. And our neighbor Peggy Dearing, a gentle woman whose two young sons are always in their backyard, playing under the great canopy of trees, flushed bright red with anger at Father Matt's scare tactics and gave him a piece of her mind.

Alas, none of us were very calm. Not good for the cause.

February 26

On Morris Lapidus, architect, from the *New York Times* obituary pages back in January. I've been carrying this scrap of newspaper around in my purse for over a month now. Morris Lapidus was born in 1902 in Odessa, Russia, came to America with his family, and was raised in Brooklyn. Here's the quote I want to savor:

> In his autobiography, *Too Much Is Never Enough,* he traces his populist style to a childhood influence—his first vision as a Russian immigrant to Coney Island's Luna Park. It was, he said, the first time he felt "an emotional surge" about architecture.

> "I was standing on the elevated platform just as dusk was falling," he recalled, "and the lights went on. To me, it was the most beautiful sight I'd seen. Of course, I knew it was hanky-pank, a circus and showmanship. But to a child of six it was all the wonders of the world. I never outgrew it."

March 1

The garden's a mess, but things are happening. Urgency rises like sap; it is time to *get down*. For instance, the little narrow bed under the front windows is clobbered with dandelions and shepherd's purse (I think that's what Martha called it, such a dainty name for such a rampant little bastard), and the rain gutter has, even in this droughty winter, gouged out its usual big hole between the two bloody tissue plants. So that's what I'd better do first. And prepare the soil for the Cecile Brunner rose I finally got my hands on. The woman at Garland said to wait a while (till mid-April) to plant it. Its roots are still young and fragile. I will be good, and wait. Bought cosmos and cornflower seeds for the front, need to go ahead and plant those. Forgot sunflowers, must get.

In the back, the daffodils are up and happy, and the crocuses already beginning to fade. I watch the dogwood daily. I want it to bloom by Passover, for Mom's visit.

What else to do? More weeding, prepare soil with lots of chicken manure and compost, plant arugula seeds and the eight million sweet peas I bought with Kris at Garland, all along the chain-link fence. Maybe lettuces in the box this time? Or snow peas? Work on the soil. Fertilize rhodies. Put slug bait around the mysteriously silent delphinium. A pure expression of tenderness, those shoots.

Meanwhile, I am learning two of the easiest of Bach's Goldberg variations on the piano—though really, none of them are remotely easy. It is both distressing and delicious to hear, in the mind's ear, Glenn Gould's interpretation behind my own halting phrases. I fear it keeps me from actually learning the note values, because his iconic interpretations—lingering in some places, radically speeding up in others—are caught so deeply in my head.

Hannah and I went downhill skiing last Saturday at Willamette Pass. She got halfway down the slope that upset her the last time she was here, the one called By George, and turned to me. "I am not going to let this defeat me," she said, with grown-up calm. And she didn't.

March 2

We are coming up on the final Planning Commission hearing on the Newman Commons. We are tired, and expect to be depressed by the experience. Our team has planned to go for a postmortem drink at McMenamins Pub.

In other news: I sowed the sweet peas along the chain-link fence, between Martha's honeysuckles and next to the *Clematis jackmanii*. Today or over the weekend I will sow cosmos, cornflower, sunflower seeds. My first chance to start early in this garden. It's worrisome, though: there is much talk of a bad drought this summer; we had virtually no winter. When Hannah and I went skiing, the reservoir near the town of Dexter was extremely low. Hannah was particularly disturbed by the exposed stumps in the lake bed.

March 7

The Newman Commons hearing was, as we'd expected, depressing, and although two commissioners expressed reservations and one tried to insert a revision bringing the building down to thirty-five feet, or three stories, in the end, all the commissioners voted for the original motion. Tina, the most vocal and feisty member of our group, wants to appeal to the City Council. But I think it's over. I find it hard to believe that we've got a chance with them. For one thing, the guy from the City Council sitting in on the planning meetings is clearly gung ho for the project. Secondly, it appears that pressure has been applied to various groups around town that would, under normal circumstances, be interested in saving the historic buildings. Carol the oceanographer told us last night that the Benton County Historical Society (and did she mean, also, the Historic Preservation Advisory Board?) were warned by the city attorney "to stay away from this one."

Ominous. Does that mean that objecting to this project would be perceived as "anti-Catholic"? What's disturbing, at the base of everything, is the way language is used to twist logic in so many different ways. For instance, our objections to the scale of the building and the destruction of historic properties has been interpreted (by Father Matt and, from there, on to God knows where) as objection to the Newman Center's mission—if you battle the development, you are perceived as battling "the good people and their good mission" of campus ministry. Is this what's called a false syllogism? The night Father Matt made this claim, I thought, naively, that he'd dug his own grave. Now I see that simply planting the seed in the commission's and the public audience's heads sent a subtle message. Guilt! Any objection will be seen as a threat to religious good works. That would frighten any local member of the church, wouldn't it? And, in fact, our friend the architect has told us that an old-time contractor in town, a man he very much respects, privately objects to the Newman Commons project but is "keeping his mouth shut" because he's Catholic.

March 12

We're going to meet with some of our neighbors to hash out the possibility of an appeal to the City Council, asking them to look again at the decision. All kinds of people who will not be affected one way or the other are telling us we have "little to lose" or "it's low risk," so we might as well go ahead. The words "little" and "low," as opposed to "nothing" or "no," worry me deeply. I am feeling extremely cautious and freaked, imagining that the developers (chiefly Father Matt) will take some sort of revenge on us. We have every right to appeal, and I must try not to feel intimidated. My guess is that when all is said and done (that is, by the deadline, Monday, April 2), we will have gone ahead and filed.

Meantime, it is raining, and lovely and quiet with the students just gone for spring break, the forsythia in bloom, tulips starting up, daffodils still hot. Rhodies and azaleas either popping or looking dangerously swollen, as if to say, "Let me out of this damn corset." I hate to leave when it's this beautiful, but I've promised my mother I'll come to Southern California for a weekend visit.

Mysteriously, the Willamette Valley is probably still in for a big drought this summer. Our friend Jeff says the snowpack at Mount Hood is half what it was last year. Hard to imagine. But anyway, it felt good to garden in the drizzle, the drow. For the record, I sowed Fordhook Favorites climbing nasturtiums in a spot we've dubbed "Hannah's rock garden," because she likes to rearrange the stones there, and I've added scarlet lobelia to the northwest back corner. If the nasturtiums don't work, it will be because the soil is too rich. That's a new concept for this novice gardener. I sowed the same nasturtiums, along with arugula, in the back-deck window boxes. We'll see. An experiment in sunlight. Be sure not to overwater that box. It apparently irks the nasturtiums. In all ways, they like to be left alone. Arugula seeds also went into the "south" lettuce bed (these names are entirely too grand for the spaces), and more scarlet lobelia seeds went into the herb bed, next to the violently rampant bee balm, which apparently I did not fully rip out.

Did I mention that T and I got married?

We did, we did. Rented the very pretty Hanson Country Inn on the edge of town, filled it with our families and friends—and, my God, almost the whole English Department showed up! The fields all around were a hectic green, spangled with sunlight and rain, and full of robins. Kris lavished the buffet table with silver stones and white narcissi she'd been forcing all winter, and Martha made a beautiful organza shawl to go with my slate-colored dress. Two of our graduate students played piano and cello. The only hiccup: the Unity minister we hired failed to show up at 1 PM for the short rehearsal he himself had suggested. We were rescued by a kindhearted professor who also happens to be a lay deacon for the Newman Center and St. Mary's Catholic Church. When at last the rather dazed-looking Unity minister showed up, a mere hour before the ceremony, we sent him packing with a strange exhilaration, and our friend the professor-and-deacon performed the ceremony with great good humor and warmth. The fact that neither of us was Catholic he quietly let slide.

Hannah was our sole attendant, a slip of a thing in dark blue velvet, preceding me down the staircase into the living room. At the moment of the kiss, with great delicacy, she held her nose and grinned out at the crowd. She brought down the house.

Spring

Capistrano Days

One swallow makes not a spring.
—Aristotle

I'm on the freeway in my native land—home to visit my mother—when on National Public Radio they announce that today, March 19, a traditional spring rite will be celebrated at Mission San Juan Capistrano. I move over into the slow lane, confused by the little rush of pride and nostalgia that besets the prodigal's return, even if it's only for the weekend. There, on the national news, as if to accuse me, is the solemn seductive ringing of the old mission bells, apparently happening right this minute, twenty miles south. How could I have ever left Southern California? And for western Oregon, my God, that fog-shrouded country to the north? Never mind: a soothing male voice begins to read aloud the story of John O'Sullivan, the Franciscan padre who used to welcome the swallows to the mission at San Juan Capistrano about a hundred years ago. "During Mass I was distracted by the noise of fluttering wings out in the little patio, and the unmistakable squeaking cry of the eave-swallows. They had come for *la fiesta de San José*, and were just in time for Mass," O'Sullivan had said.

Listening, I feel the faint new lean of my heart toward elegy, toward stories of anything beautiful and lost. It's been coming on all year, like the first twinges of stiffening joints, insomnia, and a belief in my own mortality. I am, at this very moment, forty-three years old and on my way to Goodwill Industries in a mournful, ragged mood, for my mother is at last being forced by age and finances to sell our family's house on the beach cliff, and I have been invited home to sort through the last boxfuls of adolescence and childhood. In other words: to get rid of the crap in my desk drawers, and particularly the stacks of old rock 'n' roll records moldering in the closet: Bread, Cat Stevens, Led Zeppelin, America, I can't go on. I have already been to the used-record shops, where the clerks had, without exception, thumbed rapidly through the cartons, then pushed them grimly back across the counter. "Sorry, lady," said one. "But they're all from the *seventies*."

Who, at such a juncture, trapped on the freeway with the artifacts of a discarded cultural moment, could resist a detour, turn the face briefly away from the coming dark, the shedding of earthly possessions? So what if Swallows Day is a famous tourist destination and that now, on the radio, they are acknowledging some trouble with the actual swallows? Apparently they're not coming to the mission like they used to, put off, possibly, by so much new pavement in the town, and not enough insects. There is speculation that the effort to save the old mission itself is the trouble: it was recently retrofitted for earthquake safety, and when the new roof went up, away went the swallows. Though the mission staff has been trying to woo them back with ladybugs and mud baths in the rose garden, the birds have been spotted in such unglamorous and inconvenient locations as freeway overpasses and the eaves of the new Mission Viejo mall—even in the ruins of "The Bluffs," a cluster of ten apartments that collapsed and slid down a hillside during a recent rainstorm

"A far cry from the old days," a local man is telling the reporter. He explains how the swallows used to make a thousand trips from the mission walls to the old lagoon nearby, using the local volcanic tuff and sandstone from the mission itself to build their conical nests.

Yet, in spite of all this, there remains the ringing of the mission bells for the feast of Saint Joseph—surely a testament to human hope—and the plain truth that the rainy Oregon winters and overheated classrooms of my new life have made me yearn for the salt air, the hot light of my childhood. Here on the freeway, my imagination runs rampant: in no time at all I could be sitting under crumbling adobe eaves and a cascade of purple bougainvillea, taking in that heady perfume, and also the music of the little handful of birds as they find their old nests and set about restoring them. I feel a certain kinship with these swallows: in less than three months, our old wood-frame house on the cliff will probably be purchased by a millionaire, bulldozed into oblivion, and a new house, gleaming white and palatial, will rise up in its stead, no place for nests of any kind. Even my own bedroom will go down, my west-facing room, still intact with its trashy romance novels on the bookshelves, the posters of George Harrison and the peaks of the snowy Himalayas, the green carpet faded from years of brilliant sun, where I used to lie on my belly on summer afternoons and dream.

In Los Angeles, this is a good way to have a car accident. But I can't stop dreaming, not yet. In twenty minutes, I could be well out of the clutches of Goodwill and into something approximating a ritual of old California, a glimmer of the last place I have a right to call *home*, just before it vanishes forever. Surely destiny is involved.

I telephone my mother from a gas station, tell her my plan.

A little silence greets me. "Sweetie, forget the swallows," she says at last. "They don't come back anymore. The whole thing's a myth, a tourist nightmare. Everybody down here knows it. You're only here for two days. Can't you just relax?"

Everybody down here: Is there a phrase that stings the prodigal more than this? I try to fight the feeling of doom, to remember a time when my mother and the local authorities have been proven wrong, but nothing comes to mind.

"But Mom," I reply, in my best professorial tone, and go on, more or less, in this vein: Did you know that this fiesta is possibly our region's only surviving community tribute to nature? And okay, maybe you're right—there are more tourists than swallows—but admit it, where else around here can a person find this fantastic aura of mythology and folktale, smack in the midst of this mecca of materialism? Even the spectacle of tacky souvenir kitsch might be a marvel worth witnessing, here in Orange County, which is forever trying to eradicate the affordable—as in "lower-class"—pleasures, *Mom*.

At this, another, deeper silence falls, during which I know she is holding the receiver away from her ear and gazing heavenward.

But it's too late to stop. Did you know, I say, without the slightest consideration for her feelings, that the word *kitsch* comes from the German and means, according to the Czech writer Milan Kundera, *the eradication of shit*? Still silence. But I've got her attention now, and press on, as the great trucks rev their engines behind me. I describe how, in his novel *The Unbearable Lightness of Being*, Kundera tells us— I am of course paraphrasing—that the job of kitsch is to hide the dirty truth about a culture with symbols that warm our collective hearts. We weep together at the spectacle of children playing in the grass, the sight of our own happy happy life.

"For God's sake, what's your point?" she cries. "You want the car for the day, take the car!" Then she pauses. "When are you going to tackle your room?" she says, and in her voice is a slightly worrisome tremble, the real thing. "Please don't be late. You don't know the traffic here. It's so much worse than it used to be."

"I know," I say, closing my eyes. "Thank you. Thank you." And I get back in the car, with a wild feeling of illicit freedom, more or less.

To get to San Juan Capistrano from the north, you can avoid the freeway for a few miles and take a beautiful, twisty stretch of the Pacific Coast Highway. As a sixteen-year-old with a new license, I used to drive its curves, past the tiny, funky trailer park above the beach at El Moro, and into the bohemian and romantic Laguna Beach, with its old bookstores and older cottages clinging to the hillsides. I dreamed of living in Laguna Beach the way a locked-up princess dreams of rescue, because indeed *our* town was changing fast. From the rolling hills of the former Irvine Ranch came the rumble of bulldozers, and minutes later elegant gated communities and cul-de-sacs sprang to life, everything named for something that had just gone missing: Big Canyon, Promontory Point, Jasmine Creek, stop me. But listen: in those days, cattle still dotted the grassy coastal hills south of us, and a teenaged girl could wander moodily up to her waist in high grass with her guitar to sing the saddest, most beautiful songs from the radio, and fantasize that the sad-eyed boy she liked would come upon her there and recognize a kindred, melancholy soul.

Just in that spot I now see a double phalanx of imposing palms, a lush choreography at the entrance of what will soon be an exclusive new housing development. *Newport Coast* is inscribed in tall letters on a white portico, behind which the last cows chew the last grass, once in a while gazing out at the road.

Thank God, on the ocean side of the coast highway there still stands the old Date Shake Shack. Of course it was once new, and maybe a hideous crude scar on the natural landscape, but look how it's weathered and become part of the eye's search for the familiar. OPEN SEVEN DAYS reads the sign—visible from some distance—but as I get closer, I see rough boards nailed against the old take-out windows, and turn my gaze away. Surely, farther south, the *good* kitsch will be intact, even if the swallows themselves are missing. I steel myself for the reality of no swallows and storefuls of swallow kitsch. I vow to find a way to delight in the colorful shot glasses and dusty snow globes full of swallows, the swallow pins and swallow hats, the swallow weather vanes, and possibly little plastic models of the old mission itself, all of it, if Kundera is right, designed to hide a terrible truth about us: that we can't stand our mortal nature, our muddy, defecating, decaying selves.

Even so, what is it about *old* kitsch, yesterday's kitsch, that charms us in a wistful, elegiac way? For I'm starting to mourn kitsch the way people mourn the passing of a species. I can imagine our own old beach town in the fifties, full of hats and ashtrays that said, "Surf's up!" And I've heard that inland, long ago, there was once a giant concrete orange on a highway, inviting tourists into a special orange diner where, just in front of a big old grove, you could buy your child orange-colored toothpaste and an orange-shaped pencil sharpener. It was long gone before I was born, as the orange groves of Orange County are now gone. At some point, even kitsch itself must be eradicated, lest it become an embarrassing reminder, a naked monument to the stripping away of a natural landscape, a communal memory.

But what gives me the right to get sentimental over orange groves and coastlines? I am, after all, the rootless child of a restless man, himself the descendant, he used to say with great robust pride, of the Huns, or the Mongol hordes, or whoever it was that conquered central Europe on horseback, ransacking and pillaging and doubtless performing their own acts of real estate development. Whatever instinct drives the swallows north and south, in the appointed season, drove my own father west, west, west in his. An ancient hunger was surely alive in him, that child raised in the Chicago tenements with their narrow alleyways, and their views of identical windows, identical laundry, just across. It sent him all the way here, where only the Pacific could satisfy his eye's search for the new and, maybe too, the memory's hunger for the vast and wavy steppes of a dim ancestral place.

It was my father's powerful wish that planted us here on the western verge, and so it's his ghost my mother dreads in the selling of this house. She resisted moving here from our inland town in the first place. Was it a good idea to raise children on a cliff? But he'd wanted it more than anything in the world, and my father, that Jewish ghetto boy, descendant of the Huns, who'd raised himself up from the muck American-style, was nobody you could stop.

But now, at last, finances being what they are, and my mother nearly eighty, it's perfectly reasonable, isn't it, that she should sell the beach house? She held on to it as long as she could after his death, but it's getting harder for her to go up and down the steep stairs, and, she told me carefully the night I arrived, as if my father's ghost might overhear, "Things are *starting to happen.*" By this she means *disturbances*: invasions of ants, frequently clogged sewage pipes, fractures in the picture windows from the successive thrashings of El Niños and also from the sonic booms caused by the bomb tests off San Clemente Island. And aren't we expecting a big earthquake sometime soon? She's had, all weekend, a reserved and readied look—how else to describe it?—as if she's trying not to look eroded in front of one of her children.

Even the way we call this place "the beach house" gives it a temporary feel, like a place to go on weekends and in summer. And then there's the deep embarrassment of living on an ocean cliff over a state park beach. As a teenager I tried desperately to pretend I didn't live there. The first time I came down the long flight of beach stairs in my bathing suit, I thought the whole world was staring up at me with hatred: people from inland, people who lived in lousy apartments and had exhausted themselves on the freeways, then dragged umbrellas and picnic lunches for several blocks or paid for parking in the big state-run parking lot. I never used the stairs again, but sneaked out of the house when my father—full of pride at his brilliant purchase, his *steal*—wasn't looking, straight to the beach path the inland people used.

It was only in my twenties, in that wondrous anonymity we are granted after we've officially left home—especially in a town like this, in this state, where everyone is always moving in or moving out—that I came to see how hauntingly beautiful this coastline is. Hauntingly, because of how fast the things I recognize—cling to— must necessarily vanish. In those first visits back, I practiced a new form of denial: late at night, I turned off all the lights and stood at the picture windows—a throwback to my old need not to be seen—but also because at night I could look out to sea and pretend nothing had changed. All I could see was the lighthouse light on the vast black ocean, and hear the waves pressing closer and closer to the base of the cliff, sounding hollowly under the house with a premonitory boom.

In real life, in daylight, I have arrived in San Juan Capistrano and have found, at length, a parking place along its crowded streets. The mission bells have long since been rung, but I am in time to see, lined up in front of the church, all the children of the Mission Parish School, making ready to enter the sanctuary for the special Swallows Day mass. Kindergartners in brown Franciscan habits lead off, their waists bound with rough rope belts, followed by the first- and second-grade *caballeros* in starched white shirts and black pants, then prepubescent *señoritas* in bright skirts and embroidered blouses, and, finally, the dignified Spanish aristocrats of the higher grades, with their velvet breeches and cool expressions. I follow the procession into the church, hoping to hear some Latin, a little chanting, and maybe the frantic beating of wings overhead. Alas, the music is all new folk-Christian, and there are no swallows in the eaves. The oldest thing I see, before stepping outside again, is the anachronistic solemnity of the children seated in the front pews, one hundred small friars and peasants and bewigged members of the Royal Court, all of them sweating and sitting rigidly upright, awaiting further instruction.

Still, the Mission San Juan Capistrano is a place of astonishing beauty. I can see this, even as I pay my five-dollar entrance fee into the central courtyard and present my hand for stamping with a swallow stamp. The courtyard is a real sanctuary: cool dark shelter under arched corridors, and a fine stone fountain in the center. In March, blazing in sunlight, are orange cestrums, calla lilies, blue hibiscus, and, yes, sprays of bougainvillea, purple, magenta, dark, dark red, all of it curling over the walls, and the hazy blue in the distance reminds you that the Pacific is close by. In the gift shop I find another of Charles Saunders's books, this one called *Capistrano Nights*, written in 1930, and sit down on a bench to read. This, I realize, is what the NPR host was reading from: it's full of quaint sketches and dialogues with Padre John O'Sullivan, the turn-of-the-century Franciscan father who restored the mission's neglected gardens. Near the end of the book, the padre explains how the swallows came to nest at the mission in the first place—a legend he himself seems to have created. One day he saw a hotel proprietor cursing "the dirty birds" and knocking out their nests with a pole. "The poor birds were in a terrible panic, darting hither and thither, flying and screaming about their demolished homes . . ." When O'Sullivan asked what the man was doing, the proprietor replied, "Why, these dirty birds are a nuisance, and I am getting rid of them. . . . They've no business here, destroying my property."

Saunders explains what happened next: "'Then come on, swallows,' cried the padre. 'I'll give you shelter. Come to the mission, there's room enough there for all.'" And, O'Sullivan tells Saunders, "Sure enough they took me at my word, and the very next morning they were busy building under the eaves of the restored sacristy of Father Serra's church."

I am neither a Christian nor a declared birdwatcher, but who can resist such a story—from the twentieth century, no less? I know of course that we don't communicate with the "wingeds" the way we once did. In *The Spell of the Sensuous*, David Abram recounts how the elders of an Alaskan tribe, the Koyukon, have told researchers that the robin's song is changing: "The robins don't say their song plainly anymore—they only say it halfway, like a kid would when it's learning."

Down in the lower forty-eight, we've long since lost the knack of close listening, though many people still greet the harbingers of spring with pleasure and ceremony. Every February, I've heard, rural residents in the Midwest erect poles outfitted with martin gourds to welcome back the biggest of the North American swallows, the purple martin, in a tradition that can be traced back to ancient Native American peoples. Tracy's grandfather in Oklahoma went so far as to name his returning pair Jo-Jo and Martha. Near the end of his life, dying of emphysema and no longer able to speak, he recorded *their* voices. This tape, along with a purple button that says, "IT'S PURPLE MARTIN TIME!," was a part of his legacy to his grandson. I've long envied this story: it smacks so of actual connection to actual place, and that legendary habit of elders to hand down the stories of their time—elders who, even when they lose their voices, still find a way. Maybe my own faint stirring of the blood, this desire to celebrate the spring with a lot of people, is justifiable after all, and even an ancient human need.

As I sit in the mission courtyard, peacefully drowsy with Saunders's book in my lap, a man strolls past and hands me a small newspaper. This is the special "Swallow Issue" of the mission calendar, and on its front page is a quaint legend, telling how the little birds were originally believed to travel to Capistrano from the Holy Land, carrying a twig in their beaks, which they dropped on the ocean whenever they wanted to rest from their journey. Below this is an upbeat retelling of Padre O'Sullivan's "Miracle of the Little Birds" and, in a little box, the tale of how Leon René, an American songwriter, was listening to his radio one morning in 1939 when he heard the announcer say that the swallows were returning to Capistrano, and was inspired to write his hit song.

Yet a faint disturbance lies buried deep in the promotional heart of the mission calendar: *Visitors don't seem to mind that people far outnumber the little migrating birds. They welcome them enthusiastically and stay to enjoy the all-day festivities at the Mission.*

A hearty schedule of pageantry and old-fashioned human celebratory stuff follows, though several of these events suggest a din that would discourage the most convivial swallow. The mission bells were presumably rung at 7:30 AM "the moment the first swallow is sighted," and followed, later in the morning, by a special Saint Joseph's Day Mass, during which the king and queen of the Royal Court (selected from students of the Mission Parish School) were crowned by Monsignor Paul Martin. But there is plenty still to come: the granddaughter of Leon René will sing his world-famous love song, "When the Swallows Come Back to Capistrano." Native American cooks will make fry bread, and the schoolchildren of the Mission Parish School will perform special dances. The list goes on: dancing by local Juaneño Indians and Aztec dancers from Los Angeles. *Mariachis will perform both days.*

It is an impressive array of semi-local folk custom, full of the charmingly archaic traditions of some other time, the good kitsch, after all. But there is one last item.

At 3:30 PM the U.S. Air Force Golden West Wings will perform aeronautical feats over the 221-year-old mission.

It's enough to make me bury my nose in the jasmine-scented moonlight of *Capistrano Nights* or, God forbid, agree with my mother. But here's the irony: when I go back to Saunders's book a few minutes later, I begin to see how it's pure elegy itself, mourning the lost traditions of the local Indians, these traditions themselves long since inflected with Spanish language and customs. In any case, many of the stories suggest, one way or another, that we've long since lost our gift for the right celebration of nature. The aged mission bell ringer, a Juaneño Indian called Acu, shakes his head and says wistfully to O'Sullivan, "Ah padre, the *fiestas* the Indians used to have when I was a boy. . . . Many would gather together in a circle around a fire of thick logs burning in the center. Everybody sang, each in turn, women and all; according as their turn came in the row, they would sing. The song was about the gavilan, the hawk, and how he was caught and killed, and how his wings were tied, and a thousand other things they would sing about him." Another

Capistrano resident, Doña Balbineda, echoes his cry elsewhere in the book: "*Ay, padre, qué buena música que había antes*—what good music there was in the early days!"

The good padre would probably tell me not to complain: is it not miracle enough that in the early twenty-first century, in a landscape rapidly filling in with high-priced condominiums and swanky shopping plazas, the swallows' return is celebrated at all? And—if you don't count the U.S. Air Force Golden West Wings—it is at least being celebrated in the old, human, earthbound way: with the dances of children, a procession, and a feast. But I can't help wishing I'd seen this thing before the swallows stopped coming and the Golden West Wings got in on it.

Too late: the fiesta microphone blurts on and a bright and edgy voice awakens me. "Hi, all, I'm Del Maze, your master of ceremonies." And though he is fighting a cheap sound system, I get the firm sense that he'll prevail. "The media will tell you tonight on the news that the swallows are diminishing, but I tell you they're not. The fact is, they've got more places to hang out now, and I want to personally thank the swallows for diminishing the mosquito population around my house. I like to think of them flying over my head, making their little Zorro signs in the sky."

There is a light, nervous patter of applause, and the fiesta is officially under way. It's ten in the morning and already hot. A giant swallow in a felt suit weaves sluggishly through the crowd, posing with tourists for pictures. Mission docents in shiny red bolero jackets wander the grounds answering questions with authentic patience. One of these, a senior citizen named Doris, shakes her head and recalls how it used to be: "Hundreds of nests in the mission's eaves, the feeling of wings all around you." Beside her, a representative from the Pacific Wildlife Project says, "There's just too much concrete in town now. It's tougher for them to find a home." He's handing out information sheets on swallows, with headings including "Swallow Legends" and "Swallow Facts." I learn a few things: how, in fact, the birds begin their spring migration in mid-February, in Goya, Argentina, and fly mostly at altitudes above two thousand feet, appearing to follow the valleys of the Paraná and Paraguay rivers to Lake Mirin, bypassing the Andes, and taking their valleys northward toward the Gulf of Mexico and the Yucatán Peninsula, where they turn west to the Pacific, reaching San Juan Capistrano and the agricultural valleys of California around the middle of March.

Granted, I'm more drawn to the legends than the facts. It turns out, not surprisingly, that the swallow has been encumbered with human sentiment and bizarre theories for a very long time. Our attachment to ancient notions seems particularly stubborn when it comes to these creatures. Aristotle suggested that swallows did not migrate, but tucked themselves away in the hollows of trees and under the frozen surfaces of northern lakes, to wait out winter in a torpid state. Another theorist, "a Person of Learning and Piety," proposed, in 1703, that swallows, "obviously too delicate to undertake sea crossings," wintered on the moon.

It was a fellow named John Ray, who, in the late seventeenth century wrote with consummate tact that "it seems more probable that they fly away into hot countries, viz. Egypt, Ethiopia, etc. than that either they lurk in hollow or trees, or holes of Rocks and ancient buildings, or lie in water under the Ice in Northern Countries."

But the most prominent of all the headings, the one I've been avoiding, is, ironically, right under the drawing of a swallow pursuing a flying insect. *Damage Prevention and Control Methods*. Clearly, our feelings about swallows are complicated these days, torn as we are between celebrating their ancient role as harbingers of spring and keeping them from getting too comfortable, lest they turn into a "nuisance" and a "potential safety hazard."

Up on the temporary stage, the brave festival continues. The schoolchildren have by now filed out of the church and wait, class by class, for their turn to perform. The five-year-old friars ascend the stage in their heavy brown cloaks to sing "Good Morning, Mr. Swallow." The Royal Court dances something vaguely baroque to something vaguely polka-like, while a middle-aged Davy Crockett and two Indian maidens in grass skirts and blue eye shadow stand behind tables, waiting to sell their wares: a handwoven basket, an elk whistle, a velvet painting of two Indian lovers against the ocean. Surmounting them in the sky, of course, is a pair of courting swallows.

During the Mexican hat dance, performed by somber, hot fifth graders whose blank expressions of concentration suggest that the town elders are watching them closely, closely, I give up, and escape the mission altogether. It is, I am ashamed to admit, a great relief. The real sanctuary of that day appears to be in the parked tour buses, their air conditioners running, where inside each driver reclines, solitary, his sunglasses hiding what is surely a jaded eye. One of them, his window rolled down, is singing lazily along with his radio a love song laced with new-century irony, like some answer to that swallow-inspired songwriter of old, Leon René, and his poor roped-in granddaughter, trapped now inside the mission with a microphone and the grating flare of high-pitched feedback.

It turns out I'm not alone in my desire for escape. In a nearby coffeehouse, beneath a harmonious blend of Vivaldi and state-of-the-art air-conditioning, a flock of elderly ladies has taken refuge from the heat and the long rows of Porta-Johns. These ladies are all wearing badges that read, "THE GOOD OLD DAYS CLUB." One member of the club, standing behind me in the long line for the bathroom, has strong opinions on the subject of uniscx restrooms, which lead very naturally to some thoughts on the male of the species. She leans forward conspiratorially: "Have you ever noticed the way they stink up a bathroom?" She goes on to tell me that she's a widow. "Most of us are," she adds, with a brief, wicked wink. It turns out that she used to come to the fiesta as a child, and then as a young woman. She came here every March until the day she got married. "He wasn't one for dancing," she says with a shrug. "You know, they always have some excuse."

"Were there lots of swallows then?" I ask—the topic of husbands seems faintly dangerous. She widens her eyes. "Oh, millions," she says. "Everywhere." Then, in an undertone, as if to escape official notice: "Not like now. Where would they land? Too many people. And you know what else? In my day, they didn't charge." And then, just like some eerie reincarnation of Doña Balbineda from *Capistrano Nights*, she says, "In those days, it was mostly music, and lots of dancing. We had so much fun."

Ay, Padre, it is hard to escape the vision of a wild party, men in porkpie hats tipping women backward, women whose crimson dresses attract butterflies and hummingbirds as they sway. Mariachis, yes, and all evening long, a swing band. Swallows are clearly just the beginning of this lush festival in the mission courtyard, with its central fountain, its spilling flowers and dark lovers' corners, the sacred narrative of human suffering and hope lying just behind the great walls.

As I emerge from the restroom, the widow, my Doña Balbineda, briefly takes my hands in hers and squeezes hard. "Don't forget us," she says, tapping her name badge. Her eyes go bright with rising tears, and seem oddly familiar. Who does she remind me of? I can't think, but I get a little chill, wondering who is looking out at me through those eyes. Then she vanishes into the restroom, holding her nose.

Though I haven't seen a swallow yet, something else is tugging on me now, quietly insisting that it might be time to leave. It has something to do with the widow. I look at my watch and hear my mother's voice, with that little tremble in it: *Please don't be late. You don't know the traffic here. It's so much worse than it used to be.*

Yes, it's time to go. But shouldn't I, before I depart, sample the swallow kitsch in the shops outside the mission? Maybe even bring my mother back a souvenir—though I realize, even as I think this, that it's the adolescent in me, feeling some need to prove I've been where I said I was going.

This is where I run into my final trouble. I find the kitsch all right, but not the kitsch I'm hoping for: not the old stuff, swallow snow globes, swallow buttons, and the like. It's New Age kitsch, mostly to do with angels, gargoyles, and scented candles. In shop after shop, the air is burdened with potpourri and synthesized music meant to calm. In the place of a real sky full of actual swallows, there is, over my head in one shop, a false blue sky hung with Styrofoam clouds moving across it in gentle spasms, strings of tiny Christmas lights standing in for stars. There are sweatshirts and mugs that read "Touched by an Angel."

There is, I understand, a lot of dark cultural truth needing concealment.

I am saved, briefly. For just next door to this shop is an old cantina, a holdover from the forties, dark and redolent of cheap beer, cramped as a cave and full of men. I glance in and see the faint last gleams of ancient territoriality in their eyes. There are marvelous, hostile notices thumbtacked up on a bulletin board: BEWARE: PIT BULL WITH AIDS, and so on. As I pass by, I say a little prayer: that this cantina will last a long time. Longer, anyway, than the angels.

The swallows—my God, I've forgotten to look for them. Back out on the sidewalk, I squint up into the trees, and into the eaves. Behold the pigeon, the mockingbird, and the starling. I close my eyes and imagine that the swallows are simply elsewhere and doing just fine. I tell myself they're not necessarily endangered, they've just gone somewhere practical and out of sight, where they can get the mud and insects they need. In a few years, when they see how hard the mission staff has tried to make it home for them again, they'll be back. In the meantime, maybe they're really nesting in the ruins of The Bluffs, in the eaves of the new mall, under the overpasses— though I can't help remembering something ominous and cryptic the Pacific Wildlife Project representative said to me. "With birds," he said, "sometimes it's not the obvious thing."

And I know now that it isn't only the swallows I've forgotten. With mothers, too, sometimes it's not the obvious thing. I picture her at home, waiting for my return, not in my room but in her own, among her own boxes of photographs and letters. "So much stuff," she told me when I first arrived. "I don't know where to start." As I stood there, she lifted from a box a yellowed sheet: a love letter from my father dated 1939, the year of their courtship and, I realize now, the year in which Leon René wrote his love song. In his own lyrical way, my father was begging her to take a weekend off from her dietetics studies and come visit him in Chicago. So ardent, so hard to turn down! She never could. And then she held the whole box out toward me as if she wanted me to take it out of her hands. "Do you think you'll want these someday? Because I don't even know if I can look."

"I want them," I said. And we didn't say anything more about it.

It's almost 3:30 PM and, according to the Migration and Nesting Information Sheet, that time of day when there might be a possibility of a few swallows coming out, briefly, to feed. But then again, didn't somebody schedule the air show, the aeronautic feats of the Golden West Wings, for this very time? Who is in charge of these ironies, so overstated and primitive?

That's it for me. Call it denial or sentimentality—I don't care. I want to remember, if not the sound of the swallows' beating wings, at least then the sound of mortal celebration on the ground.

As I drive out of town and north to the freeway, I find myself caught in traffic the likes of which I have never seen. Plenty of time to peer up under the overpasses. And although I see no swallows there, I am pleased when the NPR report comes on again, like a mysterious echo of the past. The mission bells—the ones I missed in the morning—are ringing out yet again, and the soothing voice begins once more to read from *Capistrano Nights*. I wait for the reality check, for NPR's on-site reporter to come in with the nitty-gritty, somebody who's taken in what really happened today, the heartbreaking mix of boosterism and ceramic angels, ladybugs and missing swallows. But no. This time, not even a mention of the trouble with the swallows. It is, perhaps, too melancholy a piece of news to offer the nation's tired commuters as they head home at last.

And so, to those who are listening, it will seem that the swallows *have* returned, that both the fiesta and the natural cycle are intact.

I find, at length, the sign for my exit and move my mother's car over, lane by lane by lane—are there really five of them?—until I'm out of there. I am on my way home in earnest now, my old room waiting, and my mother waiting, too. Who can resist looking up into the sky one last time? Though I can't see them, I can imagine the swallows hanging above me in pairs, making their little Zorro signs in the air, or making no signs at all, just trying to figure out where it might be safe to land.

Gardener's Journal

Since I've been back in Oregon, the trees have started to bloom in earnest: crabapple, cherry, pear, the works. The camellias are still at full throttle, as are the azaleas and rhodies, the tulips and candytuft, and the ground cover with delicate blue flowers I planted out front and can't remember the name of. To the right of the front steps, a miniature riot of pansies, in purple and yellow and black-purple, greets the eye, and soon, with any luck, three yellow Oriental poppies will open behind them. A surprise of hot color when we pull into the driveway. I'm eager to get more plants, but it's too early to go to Garland Nursery. There won't be much there, I'm sure. Still, Martha tells me it looked like all of Corvallis was there on Saturday. It was apparently so warm and sunny that people couldn't hold back any more.

The eye can stand only so much geometry. Well, mine, anyway. After what seems a year of contemplation of the back garden—culminating, like the flu, over the last several days when I've stared out the back window with a kind of aching self-irkedness, berating myself for lack of design sense, lack of force of character, even—I brought Martha over, gave her a very good cup of Yorkshire Gold tea, and made her look at it. Blue willow teacup held in two hands, she looked thoughtfully at the dreadful orange logs with their dreadful spikes still plunged deep into the earth, almost a year after Kris told me to yank them out with a crowbar. "Where's your shovel?" said Martha. "Let's just see if we can yank 'em up." We yanked, with hands and shovels and feet and backs, and lo, who needs a crowbar? With some heave and sweat, they came up. She had to leave soon after, but I was by then inspired, and took out all five bedfuls of logs—maybe twenty in all—and stacked them as far out of sight as I could. Going to try to unload them through the free ads in the newspaper. Martha has already composed the ad for me: "Free. Like-new landscape timbers. You haul." Makes them sound so lovely, doesn't it? Then Kris dropped by, and I made her shovel with me, and we knocked up the soil throughout the yard, got rid of weeds or at least turned them upside down, and then I telephoned the Bark Place and ordered five yards of Fertilome, mushroom compost, and dairy manure, to be delivered to our driveway Sunday at 10 AM.

April 9

Not long ago, in Vancouver, B.C., on our honeymoon, I ran across a handsome little paperback that cost a fortune, and that T bought for me in that way he does, when I'm maundering over a book—it feels like a ritual now. And this one, my God. It's by Ann Cline, a professor of architecture at Miami University in Oxford, Ohio, and is called *A Hut of One's Own*. A true find. First-person scholarship, with passion and voice and zero academic jargon, though I feel deeply unlearned and can read only a few pages at a time. But it is, as Ann Cline puts it, "a stroll through the borderlands that surround Architecture." The chief draw for me is her idiosyncratic delight in the pleasure and significance of a little dwelling "intensely inhabited." Randomly flipping through the book in the shop, I was startled and thrilled to come across references to M.F.K. Fisher, to childhood memories and Mississippi juke joints, Japanese tea ceremonies and "little houses of pleasure"—those garden follies where rich French counts apparently took virtuous maidens in the eighteenth century for the purposes of seduction. Apparently, after you'd been squired through the garden and into the vestibule, you more or less fell into the count's arms.

The word *vestibule* alone makes me weak in the knees.

There's a subject lurking in here somewhere for me, in my daily life and in my writing one—I don't know why I think of them as separate. Could the hut dweller's sense of scale, of the poetry of the miniature domestic space on some kind of edge of nature, help me fuse them? Cline's book resonates with M.F.K. Fisher's sensibility, with images of potager gardens and the naïf tradition of painting. And kitsch, too. No—not exactly kitsch, but folk art made with the materials at hand, and with a passion born of not yet knowing the "proper" way.

The desire to live in a state of semi-primitive poetry is so obviously a reaction against the way things are speeding up out in the world, technologically speaking, that it's almost comical. It would be, I suppose, if it didn't feel so deeply like a necessary resistance. I'll be less vague another day. After the soil's warmed up some.

In any case, I am going to write the architecture professor a fan letter. Furthermore, I'm going to ask her to read at Oregon State, either this spring or next fall. She writes, "As often happens in my life, the right book came my way just when I needed it: Kakuzo Okakura's *The Book of Tea*." This has happened to me, in spades, with *hers,* and I wonder if it might resonate with other people around here. A hunch.

Of course, a lecture on architecture isn't, strictly speaking, an English department kind of thing. If by some miracle she says yes, I'll have to find funding elsewhere on campus, God help me.

April 12

Five-thirty AM I have an hour before Hannah rises for school; what can I do in that time? Here's T's dream, which fascinated me this morning: the two of us are in a huge surging crowd attending a speech by President Bush, who is delivering it terribly, in a monotone. T turns to me and says, "He's butchering that speech." A moment later the crowd surges forward, and someone stabs the president. In the dream, T turns to me. "It's okay," he says. "It was just below the heart."

We did a groggy two-second analysis. T said, with a laconic smile, "It's probably not about Bush." We are both apprehensive about testifying, opening up this whole appeal in front of the City Council, when we feel there's not much support from the community. Our little band of eight or ten feels absurdly tiny and strident. Will the whole town be glaring at us? Will Father Matt come down from Portland? Will we feel as if the City Council is deeply bored with our complaints?

April 20

Another dream of T's I feel I must record. These are all happening in and around the time of the public hearings on the Newman Commons development. In this one, he and I are at the beach, sitting at a kitchen table in a little cottage, talking. Atmosphere of comfort, peace, very pleasant, he says. Then he looks up to see that behind me, in the picture window, an enormous wave is rising up out of the sea. Dream ends.

April 25

The pink dogwood in the backyard has bloomed. Hannah wants a color photograph of it for her school project: a real estate brochure inviting people to colonial Virginia. There is some dark irony in this I am not in a mood to explore. Went out to weed instead. It is a kind of intimate nightmare. From a distance, the mounds of Irish moss and blue star creeper look deliciously smooth—and it is true, they are growing fast, really filling in. But get up close, and there are claws of tough grass and shepherd's purse and dandelions sprouting up absolutely everywhere. It reminds me of writing. Makes me want to dig up that quote from Flannery O'Connor, something about writing being a dirty business; that you need to be willing to get your hands dirty.

Found the quote, and of course it's much better than that: "Fiction is about everything human and we are made out of dust, and if you scorn getting yourself dusty, then you shouldn't try to write fiction. It's not a grand enough job for you."

And oh, Ann Cline has written back, a long, luscious letter, and is thrilled to be invited to give a lecture here! We are in e-mail contact now, and she says she is happy to come to Oregon State this spring, and not wait until fall. Nor does she care about money: she'll come for airfare and a place to sleep. I am amazed—and the Spring Creek Project, an interdisciplinary program run through the Philosophy department, is willing to pay her travel expenses. We are aiming for early May, although in some moment of local cosmic irony, all hotel rooms are sold out for that weekend, due to the annual campus ritual called "Moms Weekend." We will figure it out.

She writes, at the end of her cheerful, vivid letter, "Be aware, however, that I'm slightly crippled . . . variously diagnosed as multiple sclerosis or stroke, neither of which I accept. It means I can't walk very far and while I speak I must be seated. . . . The mind still works, however slowly!"

In the meantime, the pink-and-white Sensation Mix cosmos have emerged, only to be promptly eaten by slugs. Will start a new batch of seeds, this time in trays. Two exquisite lavender-blue irises have opened. Others are about to pop. Azaleas and rhodies still in full wampus, and tulips, too. And there is nothing like the delicacy of that pink dogwood.

April 26

Okay, it's done. We've made our case to the Corvallis City Council. The Newman Commons development will be deliberated on Monday, April 30. At the hearing, our team was very good— everyone was well-prepared and coolheaded. And the town mayor, who ran the meeting, was marvelous; she kept wittily but firmly telling the emotional local contingent who spoke in favor of the project that their testimony was irrelevant. Spookily, the Wilsons sat right behind us in the meeting room and barely acknowledged us when we turned around to say hello. We can't help but think that they knew about the project when they sold us the house—we've heard that they know Father Matt personally. Well, that's beside the point, I guess. Realistically, we know we are going to lose the battle, but we *did* exhaust the developers and the Portland lawyers; gave them an unexpectedly tough run for their money! T turns out to be very good at parsing the city codes and ferreting out their ambiguities. It's all that close reading he did as an English major from way back. A couple of City Council folks have encouraged him to apply for the Planning Commission once this is all over. He's intrigued, and is going, tonight, to a "Citizen Involvement Meeting" to check it out. Between fighting the development and teaching, he's not getting much writing done, but he feels he has something to contribute. His love of public citizenship—in such startling contradiction to his intensely private nature—is a seed that wants to grow. Here in a town where at first he thought there was nothing to fight for, he has found something. And of course now we both see how much is going on here, all around us, all the time. A local school has closed down; one of the main industries in town is in financial trouble. And developers are always here, circling the old-fashioned downtown district in search of vacant, vulnerable buildings. We shall see.

April 28

Got up again at 5:30 AM. Two dreams, Hannah's from a few days ago and T's, from last night.

Hannah (who has been watching the Anne Frank biography on television) dreams that Hitler is still alive, though, as she puts it, "Not troubling anyone anymore, just a normal-looking person who lives now." He still lives in his house, but it's been turned into a museum, and you go up a long spiral staircase to get into his living room, where he is sitting in a chair, asking his wife a question. "Somehow I got upstairs," Hannah says, "I'm the only person who gets to go up there . . ." and then she can't remember any more.

T dreams that he is in the Wilsons' new house, and that he and Mr. Wilson are talking to each other quite cordially, but with lots of tension under the surface. In the room is a closet, and in the closet is an enormous iron safe, wide open, and T catches a glimpse of it. Mr. Wilson sees him looking and shakes a finger at him. "If I *ever* find anything missing from that safe, I'm calling the police on *you*."

April 30

Took Hannah horseback riding at a place south of town (found it in the phone book). When we got there, I discovered that the stables are on the site of a former, and recently busted, methamphetamine lab. A big extended family runs the place now, for an absentee owner, very rich. It's a beautiful piece of land: sixteen hundred acres in the foothills of the Cascades, lush cattle country. The family's twelve-year-old daughter served as our guide and told us, in a very somber, grown-up voice, "We're trying to get its reputation back after the meth lab disaster." Hannah was as fascinated by the dribs and drabs of the story as by the horseback ride itself. When we got back to the barn, she wanted to know where the "M" place was—she'd only picked up fragments as we rode. The girl pointed out the ruined blue cabin that had been the lab, as well as a big but unfinished playhouse the previous managers—the meth makers—had been erecting for their own young daughter. This is what sticks with me: the place was rife with drugs and weapons, too, and they had a little girl here, were building her a playhouse. What will Hannah remember?

May 1

Last night the City Council upheld our appeal. What this actually means is that the developers will have to stay within the neighborhood's scale as they build. So their monstrous brick building is out of the picture. We are exhilarated, but nervous, too: there's no telling what will happen next. But we all went out afterward for a celebratory drink at McMenamins Pub, and the atmosphere was giddy; we wolfed down French fries, drank beer. T is genuinely elated—what a sight! A kind of lightness in his body—he's back to full strength, albeit with a hint of disbelief still in his face. He said, lifting his glass with wicked gusto, "Now we're really in deep shit." This is the essence, somehow, of a "victory" of this nature: it means a continued involvement, a deeper one than we've even experienced so far, and more negotiation.

But what an extraordinary moment it was, as each councilperson in turn was asked for "yay" or "nay" on the appeal, and the two who'd remained silent during the debate came up "yay." A collective sigh rippled through our whole row, as if through a single organism. In the two front rows, the head attorney from the Portland legal team was looking at Father Matt, whose head and neck remained rigid. Chris, the architect we've liked all along, was shaking his head back and forth. It was the first time I've seen him display his feelings. Afterward, coming out of the ladies' room, I nearly ran into him. But he brushed past me, wouldn't look me in the eye. For my own part, I felt like running out of there. A sense of overexposure, very uncomfortable. That was bothering T, too; one of the first things he said was, "Oh my God, everybody knows where we live."

So, just as T has gotten back his health and vigor, it seems we've invited a new suspense into our lives. The lawyers and Father Matt, as we left, were huddled in a conference room upstairs in the Corvallis fire station.

What will they decide to do? Appeal to LUBA, the state's Land Use Board of Appeals? Or redesign the building yet again, with the neighborhood scale in mind? In the meantime, we fantasize about approaching the local Newman Center folks, asking them if they'll let us help—fund-raising, physical labor, anything they want—to restore the original cottages and help them get the simple thing they wanted in the first place: a better facility for their events and services. Is this a pipe dream? When should we approach them? Carol thinks we should wait a few days. But when we asked a planning commissioner what he thought, he encouraged us to "do it right away."

We got home at midnight and stood at the back window awhile, looking out at the trees in the dark, lit magically from beneath by little floodlights and heavy with green. I have invested these innocent trees with gratitude. They will waver in our skylight for one more summer now.

Chocolate and Cigarettes

She arrives in a wheelchair, appearing at the threshold of the sterile, narrow Jetway. She holds in her lap a small overnight bag, and grips in one hand a cane. In her last letter before traveling, she said, referring to the author photograph in her book, "I look pretty much the same as in the picture, only a little heavier, hair a little gray." But I don't notice either of these things. What I see is a pair of brilliant dark eyes and a calm, ecstatic expression, framed by short dark hair. If there is gray in it, I don't see it. Colette in her later years. Ann Cline is in her late fifties, if I remember from her brief biographical note, and there is on her face a look of dreamy alertness both childlike and wise. Almost immediately, we are chattering away, as if we are old friends catching up after a long separation.

On the drive down to Corvallis she tells me more about the illness. "They've diagnosed it as MS, but I don't think it is, and anyway, what good does it do to think of it this way? Forget the name, forget the diagnosis, I just think of it this way: so I need to stop and rest after walking fifty feet or so." It happened, she says, just after she finished the publication process for *A Hut of One's Own*— apparently much harder than writing the book itself. She had some kind of "collapse," and was never the same after. It remains a mystery, one she has decided to shrug off.

We discover odd coincidences that heighten the sense of magic and deep familiarity. Among other things, it turns out that she was building her first hut in Davis, California, during the years I was an undergraduate there. She recognizes the name of my beloved writing teacher. It's bittersweet to me, the way we don't meet people in one moment of our lives, but then, by some odd alchemy or accident, we do, later.

And then there is her calm gusto, which seems to bubble up from a spring of peaceful sociability, a generous heart. Insouciant and spiritual all at once. She's been told to stop smoking, of course, and to avoid chocolate, but she says, laughing, "I can't." So over the four days of her visit, we do a lot of this: between my classes and ferrying Hannah and all the little things that make a life, we find time to sit on the back deck, staring together into the garden and talking, talking, talking. T and I have lately noticed a water stain developing in the corner of our dining-room ceiling, and once, in the middle of a conversation, Ann gazes back up at the house, and says, with a meditative smile, "Don't wait too long to get that roof fixed." She smokes her cigarettes, and we talk about childhood, garden follies and teahouses, writing and books, the Newman Commons project. We even get onto the subject of "bringing" the kitchen back to its Craftsman roots. The Wilsons updated in the seventies, and it's the one room in the house that has lost all connection with the original: fake wood flooring, fluorescent lighting, and a butcher-block island we are always crashing into as we try to cook together. Ann has some thoughts on lighting design for the space and knows a good source for reproductions of Craftsman fixtures.

She even loves the shabby Twin Peaks–like motel I found for her, where no self-respecting mothers of OSU students will stay this Moms Weekend. She needed a ground-floor smoking-allowed room—not too many of those left in our town. She savors everything, right down to the cheap paneling, the peppery smell of smoke and wet dog in the carpet, and the sad-faced manager, harried by the tiny buzzing fan in his cardboard office. She strikes me as an example of Natalia Ginzburg's "recording angel." It's the elegiac sense with which she takes everything in. Like the corona of light around an eclipse.

A further surprise: when we arrive in the Memorial Union meeting room I reserved for her lecture, the place is packed to the gills. The fire marshal is there, looking very grim: we are over capacity. Among our own students and faculty and people from the community is a contingent of architecture graduate students from the University of Oregon, an hour south. There are people literally sitting at her feet, gazing up into her beatific face with its faint air of delighted wickedness. The only negative comment I hear is from a local architect, who will tell me afterward that the slow pace of her delivery and the way her thoughts meandered made him impatient. This, in fact, is the thing I most relish. In the spaces between phrases, as she pauses and considers, there is room to dwell, a fine suspension for us all.

I think she has that quality called *jen* by the Confucians. She writes about it in *A Hut*: that "delicate balance between sociability and faithfulness to oneself . . . *jen* is neither opinionated, dogmatic, obstinate, nor egoistic." Grace under pressure.

A few days later, she must go home. She has met our friends and several colleagues, eaten wild-caught salmon with them in our dining room in the evening light, spent hours on the back porch. We don't want her to leave, and she seems genuinely reluctant to go, though I know she must be exhausted. As I drive her out of town, and across the Willamette River toward the freeway and back up to the Portland airport, the sky is an insane depth of blue, the sunlight glittering on every tree and blossom as if in collusion with me—oh, stay here with us a bit longer! It's like one of those rich French counts, escorting an unsuspecting maiden through the gardens of a *petite maison*. The weather itself is trying to weave a spell around her.

As we cross the river, she turns to me with a smile.

"If heaven isn't like this," she says with a sigh, "I ain't going."

After I drop her off at the airport, I linger in the city. At Powell's City of Books I buy a postcard to send her—it seems to leap to my hand. It's the Edward Hopper painting of a country gas station, with its three red gas pumps and lone, half-obscured attendant. Only half of the station house itself is visible: a little white cottage with a red roof and delicate red cupola. But it's the way the eye is pulled to the narrow space between the building and the gasoline pumps, pulled down a bit of road and around a corner into a dark mass of trees, that calls up everything for me. The journey. The lost domain. A small dwelling place on the edge of the unknown. I scribble a note of thanks to Ann, ending with "I see a long journey," a phrase we bandied back and forth while she was here, laughing and mock-prophetic. I walk around the Pearl District, the old warehouse district just south of downtown, being renovated these days into tall condo buildings and upscale restaurants, and notice something I haven't seen before: a small corrugated tin hut snugged on a warehouse rooftop between two new sleek high-rises. I keep looking, and wake up to the beauty of cream-colored smokestacks rising above the ornate rooftops of Portland's Chinese Garden. A high-rise window composed of two tall panes goes blue-pink, like the early evening sky.

Back home, I stay out in the garden as long as I can. Sow seeds for tall black Watchman hollyhocks along the northern fence. And sunflowers, Mammoth, I think they're called. My mother thinks sunflowers are crass. Wait till she sees mine, not to mention the tea table grown over with moss I'm contemplating under the blue spruce. A daughter gone mad, back to peasant status.

A few days after her visit, I get a letter from Ann. She writes, "Somehow I fear putting pen to paper may wake me from the dream—the dream of wild salmon I can still taste . . . the dream of sixty people smiling, approving, of cappuccinos here and there and best of all, of talk without end."

Her last two sentences read like a blessing. "Keep fixing the roof," she writes. "It shelters a magical story."

I try to stay in the dream too, by reading John Berger's essay "The Ideal Palace" in *Keeping a Rendezvous*. Palaces of kitsch, gardens of obsession. Is this related to her work on little dwellings, intensely inhabited? Berger writes about "peasant palaces," kingdoms of the naïf, built with no money but with found objects (shells, sea glass, bits of broken china collected by friends and neighbors—for they, too, need this eccentric collection to exist). Each object is thus attached to a story, or vice versa. Every shard of glass. Berger tells the story of a nineteenth-century French rural postman named Ferdinand

Cheval who spent thirty-three years building his "palace passing all imagination." He quotes Cheval's own account:

> A country postman . . . I walked each day from Hauterives to Tersanne—in the region where there are still traces of the time when the sea was here—sometimes going through snow and ice, sometimes through flowers. What can a man do when walking everlastingly through the same setting, except to dream? I built in my dreams a palace passing all imagination, everything that the genius of a simple man can conceive—with gardens, grottoes, towers, castles, museums, and statues: all so beautiful and graphic that the picture of it was to live in my mind for at least ten years. . . .
>
> When I had almost forgotten my dream, and it was the last thing I was thinking about, it was my foot which brought it all back to me. My foot caught on something which almost made me fall: I wanted to know what it was: it was a stone of such strange shape that I put it in my pocket to admire at leisure. The next day, passing through the same place, I found some more, which were even more beautiful. I arranged them together there and then on the spot and was amazed.

Yes. *What can a man do when walking everlastingly through the same setting, except to dream?* I am beginning to understand this mad love for the garden and house, the life we are building within it. I want to be surprised by color and beauty and form. To make, but not too perfectly. And to recognize that beneath that urge lies something deeper than our fear of death: a fear of spiritual poverty, of being *uninhabited* ourselves. For are we not, ourselves, little landscapes, vessels in which things are constantly undergoing the process of creation and destruction?

And as if they, too, are ready to be awakened and named and inhabited for a season, now and only now do Kris's magnificent irises begin to open. She stands in our garden, her dark blue cap pulled down over her pale, wispy hair, and though I know this is happening over a great stretch of days, it all seems one moment, the moment the petals unfurl, and she recognizes them, and calls out their names.

Blue Ruffles, Song of Norway, Midnight Majesty.

Gardener's Journal

And then one day, the meditative phase ends. Just like that. Once more I am on a tear, a roar, a frenzy, a spree. Oh, I mother my child, teach my classes, dabble at my desk here and there for a minute. But mostly, I am *out there* now. I have taken off my gloves and dug in. Removing the logs was the thing. It loosened my corset, unleashed God knows what. I cannot stop planting, and today Martha and I are going to Nichols Garden Nursery in Albany, so it's not over, not by any means.

Without further ado, a list of recent acquisitions.

Back garden first:

Two clamshell-backed fifties' lawn chairs, one tomato red, the other ocean-liner white (with rust drips). Twenty-two dollars apiece at a local antiques store. In Portland these puppies go for a hundred dollars. I am well pleased.

Kris has brought me some bags of blue and green sea glass and broken china. She has a vision for the Knight Gardener shrine and begins by taking a small fine brush and some henna to his beaky face. Under her hand he is beginning to look like a god. Pan. Bacchus. Coyote. Shades of John Berger's obsessed postman, with his stones of strange shape.

Under the blue spruce in the dry shade, columbines: white Nana Alba, pink-red Granny's Bonnet. Two bleeding hearts, one pink and one "old-fashioned" white. Also tucked a bit of baby's tears and Irish moss directly under the tree. Please let them live. Oh, and Himalayan blue poppies, from seed. I should have started these in January, indoors. If they don't come up, I'll try again next year, the right way.

In the Virgin Bed: alpine poppies, more blue star creeper. Some wildflowers and orange and yellow cosmos from seed. Two peonies have popped up back there, too. From whence?

Under the pink dogwood, some woolly thyme, and out a little, two Japanese anemones. By the bird bath, more Irish moss and baby tears. Two other kinds of thyme near the herb bed: nutmeg and white creeping.

A while back in the Most Sun Bed I planted seeds for bushy Spacemaster cucumbers and early Scarlet Globe radishes. Lettuce, broccoli, plenty of arugula, and Quinault everbearing strawberries. I searched high and low for Martha's favorite, the popular little Tristar, which she says is not overly sweet and produces all summer long: she loves to go out into her garden every morning and pick just a little handful for breakfast. But the Quinaults will have to do for now; she assures me they'll be delicious, too.

The Mammoth sunflowers near the chain-link fence have germinated, popped up their tough little heads.

There is a story behind these sunflowers. A dear family friend from back East, for our wedding, nestled a packet of them into a box with a grapefruit knife and a little note. It's the knife, actually, that has the story. According to the note, my mother apparently used it in her New York City hotel room, back in the fall of 1977, when Dad was getting treated for leukemia at Sloan-Kettering. Mom gave this friend the grapefruit knife when she and Dad came home to California, a month before he died. Now the friend wants it to come back to us. An amazing wedding gift, that little knife, and sunflower seeds.

June 1

Before I forget: ever since we won the appeal from the City Council, there has been an eerie silence from Father Matt, the architects, and now the local Newman Center Board folks themselves. In the days right after the decision, T and I (and Trish and Carol, too) had positive encounters with members of the local Newman board: they seemed quite willing to talk, and to accept our help in trying to shape something that would be both compatible with the neighborhood and save the historic cottages. Then silence fell. A palpable shift. And the Newman Center Board president, with whom Trish had arranged a meeting, canceled without giving a reason. Didn't *postpone*. The atmosphere's gone conspiratorial. I'm not surprised by the Portland archdiocese's silence (i.e., Father Matt's). After all, from his point of view, silence is probably an act of dignity—the only response to our absurd objections! But does he really have so much power as a lawyer-developer that the Newman Center can't make its own decisions? Or would they rather not have to make this one? Are they, in some way, more trapped than we are? Is it only by working with Father Matt that they'll get the space they need, for worship and activities? I wonder. In the newspaper, just a few days ago, they were quoted as saying, "No hard feelings with the neighbors" and "We're back to the drawing board." Still, we worry. It's going to look mighty suspicious if, in a month, demolition begins without a peep. So much for neighborliness.

June 3

T and I walked around downtown with Kris in the late afternoon, went out for an early dinner, and from there to her studio to see her new paintings. I told her I thought Matters of Life and Death was not too much as a title for the series. The paintings are richly colored, terrifying: still lifes with tumors, pliers, corpuscles, and banana leaves. With those weird drips of hers. She is truly great; she has turned her illness into art. One painting looks like a nightmare version of tree peony buds. It is, in fact, a cell gone cancerous.

She's going to call it *Stricken Melanocytes*.

June 5

Five-thirty AM. Here I am at the desk at first light, muzzy-minded, but I have my cup of coffee, and Katia is up, too, in the window.

She slept curled up against my abdomen last night, precisely on the spot where it hurt most from cramps. My periods have gotten heavier this year. Is something up? In her late forties my mother had two big fibroids and a hysterectomy. Could this be what's keeping me from getting pregnant? Might (sigh) have to check in with the doc.

Where was I? Ah, yes. Read from my work last night at the University Club in Portland, a very swanky turn-of-the-century men's club now open to women. Very *smoking jacket* and *discreet* in tone, and no denim allowed. There was an old waiter in a red vest, tall and thin and stooped, with a cavernous face, who is apparently a Portland legend: a Holocaust survivor, he used to work at Dave's Deli, once read astrological charts in the basement of a Victorian house in Portland, and apparently rarely speaks now. Learned all this at supper from the owner of the Looking Glass Bookstore. After the reading, the old waiter came up to me and shook my hand, and thanked me for "sharing my words." He looked at me so intently I felt a shock—so much history hidden behind that gaze. And the sheer surprise of his *speaking*.

At the club, we also met a lawyer who works for the firm employed by Father Matt. He said, with a knowing smile, "Oh, I've heard all about you guys." God knows what they say in their office about these small-town maniacs.

Speaking of Father Matt, we have at last seen the new design for the Newman Commons and are heaving a collective sigh of relief—for now. The new building will be two stories tall instead of four and will run along the west side of the property, well away from Monroe Street. The courtyard with its big trees will be spared, as will three of the five cottages, including the beautiful Hillside, which faces Monroe with its mullioned windows and quirky corners. Those three houses will be restored, we're told, their interiors mostly gutted but the exterior Craftsman character kept intact. The two houses slated for demolition are the little one called Tento and the slightly larger one Snell herself lived in, which she called Bryerly (and which is known as Snell House these days). Ironic, that the one she actually lived in will be demolished, but given that *none* of the houses were ever protected by historical status, we count ourselves lucky. The new building will be set well back from the street, behind the courtyard, and have sixteen student apartments instead of sixty-four, a new chapel, and lots of Craftsman details to match those of the older buildings.

Underground parking, all flowing out onto the back street, Jackson.

The whole thing's a minor miracle.

June 7

I bought a baby lemon tree, and put it in the beautiful Vietnamese green clay pot T and I bought in Vancouver on our honeymoon. It's on the kitchen table—the "greenhouse corner," as we think of it, overlooking the backyard. Katia is very interested in it, when she's not busy eating T's beautiful funky tropical tree. He doesn't know what it's called. But it's been through everything with him: divorce, remarriage, and now this cat.

Need more stepping stones, a hose house, a washer for the hose attachment. Another window box. Five feet by twenty inches—there's a bizarre size.

June 8

Got the window box this morning. Also planted cilantro, French thyme, a huge garage sale lily, pale pink dianthus, another Sun Gold tomato, snapdragons, and three more honeysuckle starts from Martha, who dropped over for lunch. "There's more where that came from," she said. "Just let me know." Lemongrass, and a ground cover with deep purple flowers—can't remember its name, and I threw out the tag. I'm losing track—a sign of madness. I resisted buying a cardoon: it looks like it might get bigger than the whole bed. I will eventually succumb to it. How can I not? It is a cousin of the artichoke and was preferred by the Proust family cook. But where to put the damn thing? I murmured my fears to Martha and after lunch we went out back and took a look. "Nothing to be afraid of," she said. "We'll go buy it together." She lifted one hand to her forehead in the strong early summer light and smiled. "It'll transform the garden. Give it a focal point."

A gratifying prospect.

Summer
2001

Gardener's Journal

W̶e are done teaching until fall; Hannah has one more week of fourth grade. This morning, after five, maybe six days of rain and wind and heavy overcast, I woke up to see blue, real blue, behind the elm in the skylight. It was six forty-five. T had already been up for two hours, writing. I found myself flung sideways across the bed in my morning laziness. Hannah came in, dressed for her school field day in shorts and a T-shirt, with leftover fuzzy braids, but nevertheless wrapped up in a blanket. She lay down on the bed, looked up into the skylight, and said, "Look, it's almost amber!" Where does she learn these words? After I got her off to school, I pottered about in the garden a few minutes and an hour vanished, of course. I disapprove of my own methods, both as a gardener and as a writer, but they seem unbreakable. I putter, make little gestures in a disorganized way, almost half asleep, and *eventually* (I use the word advisedly) something appears: a patch clear of weeds, a row of lettuces, a rosebush in bloom. Here, too. It's a disconcerting way to work: it produces, but with a slowness that discourages me sometimes. Other times I don't like it simply because it isn't the proven way to produce. Every writer I know who is truly dedicated and productive and at the top of his or her form writes every day, usually at dawn. Nobody pulls weeds, a few at a time, plants one thing, then walks away.

In spite of my lack of discipline, the garden, at least, is looking very luscious. I seem to have planted red things in little unexpected spots between mainly blues, purples, and yellows, so every once in a while, there's a hot flare in your eye when you look out: paprika yarrow, the Don Juan rose, bee balm, Kris's penstemon in a pot, and my favorite, a violent little explosion of dianthus between a silver thyme and a lemon thyme. I got lucky; the truth is, I planted this triad rather too close together. But it appears not to matter—the thymes are, like the lavender and the yarrow behind them, extremely happy here. Martha says, "They don't need nutrition." This valley is, I guess, their Provence.

June 16

A few nights ago T, myself, and our friend Ehud volunteered as servers at Stone Soup, the soup kitchen at St. Mary's Catholic Church, a few blocks away. Every second Thursday, the Jews and Quakers are in charge. The three of us were stationed out on the gymnasium floor behind the milk, lemonade, and coffee, waiting for people as they came to the end of the food line. I love the big industrial church kitchen: all that stainless steel, the enormous burners, the walk-in fridges and freezers, the dishwasher square and silver and steaming. Such a big, good feeling there. When it's time to serve, someone in the kitchen presses a button, and voila, up lifts the slatted metal tambour door between kitchen and gymnasium, revealing the evening's casserole and soup in their steam pans, and also the food servers, spatulas and ladles aloft. What a pleasure to see T planted so sturdily behind the milk jugs in his white apron, his gentle vitality fully restored.

It was a pearl gray sort of evening outside, and a soft light filtered in through the high gymnasium windows, lighting the men and women as they sat down to eat. I recognized one man from Junior's funeral service last year: a former physics PhD candidate at OSU, I'd heard. At the long tables, people sat together in groups even if they weren't talking; an impression of momentary ease and sociability. There are clear solitaries, even in the midst of the groups: a man in a headband read an old, curled-up *McCall's,* and the one child in the room—wearing a pink snow jacket though it was June—cried off and on. An older gentleman who, in the late afternoon, had helped us set up the tables, was overtaken by twitching: he crushed his hands between his legs, put his thumbnail to his mouth and bit hard, moved his arms in a rapid sequence, then started over again, in order.

People drank lots and lots of milk, very little coffee or lemonade. But milk—it looked like it satisfied. Everyone ate hard—how else to put it? Seriously bent over their plates of curly noodles and meat sauce, salad and bread and pea soup. They whispered jokey complaints to us as we poured the milk—"The food's so bad it'll make your hair fall out"—but the truth is, everyone was chowing down, coming back for seconds, even thirds, and then walking out with containers of leftovers and loaves of bread donated by the local grocery store. I'd love to cook here sometime (the cooks start at one-thirty in the afternoon). Could one make Mrs. Rodriguez's tacos, with avocado and stewed tomatoes and cumin in the ground beef, for seventy? Is that too ambitious?

Garden stuff: chicken manure and compost are not the same thing, goddamn it. My education continues. You can't let the manure—or even some of these really rich plant composts—touch the base of the plants. They'll turn them to toast. You must add them to other soil first, then leave a bit of room around the plant's base. All this I learned in the nick of time, asking some other aimless question at Garland. Such horror on the employee's face, as she realized I'd dropped chicken manure on my roses' feet.

As a rule, when people tell you what to do, they only tell you half of what you need to know. You find out the other half later, by accident.

June 17

I believe I failed to mention that neither the black hollyhocks nor the Himalayan blue poppies made it. I will try again next year, much earlier, in the windowsill, if I can persuade Katia not to eat them or lie down on them. The "greenhouse window" is her preferred sunning and bird-watching spot in the kitchen. Because of the traffic out on Monroe Street, we have kept her indoors, and she has rights to every window in the house now.

June 20

From the "chronicle" that accompanies Rainer Maria Rilke's *Letters to a Young Poet*, translated by M. D. Herter Norton:

> To write rhythmic prose one must go deep into oneself and find the anonymous and multiple rhythm of the blood. Prose needs to be built like a cathedral; there one is truly without a name, without ambition, without help: on scaffoldings, alone with one's consciousness.

June 23

Went to a dinner party in the hills of Eugene. I think Edith Wharton would have had a field day analyzing it, and Chekhov would have quietly taken these lives apart. The privileged female scientist who incessantly ripped on Texas, whose blue eyes snapped with repressed anger. At what, I wonder. The sweet and anxious hostess whose dinner preparations—lamb, roasted potatoes with rosemary, a lovely salad, a marionberry pie—were wonderful but somehow made me sad. She kept saying what she *would* have done, if she'd had time, such as "a little reduced wine sauce for the lamb," when in fact she and her husband were clearly proud of their efforts. She listed the ingredients of her salad dressing in a way that was, I think, intended to convey its simplicity, its peasant nature, but in fact spoke of effort, of the need to *tell*, not to mention the need to use two different kinds of vinegar! I have, I'm afraid, been guilty of this myself; it seems to come along with the summertime riches of this valley. We wind up bragging about having the freshest ingredients, the rosemary from our own yard, the raspberries from the local farmers' market, and I hear, in my own voice, an anxiety I can't quite place. Is it that we are, in fact, embarrassed to be living in what Portlanders call "the provinces"? The embarrassment of urbanites who have, for job or kid raising or perhaps exhaustion, fled the big city? Must we display to each other, somehow, that we haven't lost our sophistication? But doesn't that destroy the whole notion of true sophistication? Kris is not this way; nor is Martha. These are imaginative, skilled cooks; the difference is simply that they don't go on neurotically about what they do. Well, they will explain something if you ask, which I do, but with a kind of low-key offhandedness that bears its enthusiasm with dignity. And my student Tanya is another matter altogether: she is a cooking artist and talks about it with that peculiar, slightly mad excitement of the artist. I can only pray that in the future I learn to keep my mouth shut when I'm serving up dinner. And be less agitated when I do it. I know I make a show and an unholy mess. To quote M.F.K. Fisher about her friend Sue, who had, it seems, that quality called *jen* that Ann Cline wrote about, and has herself:

> [S]he nourished herself and many other people for many years, with the quiet assumption . . . that man's need for food is not a grim obsession, repulsive, disturbing, but a dignified and even enjoyable function. Her nourishment was of more than the flesh, not because of its strangeness, but because of her own calm.

A Kitchen Odyssey

The kitchen, . . . a self-contained world, has a distinct set of rules and sense of place. There are many that would name it as their favorite room in the house.
—Paul Duchscherer and Douglas Keister, *Inside the Bungalow*

There is nothing quite like a charming old house with a kitchen *overhauled* in the seventies. Whole rooms may escape unscathed, but rarely the kitchen, no matter what good principles it was born with. When it comes to kitchens, are we more susceptible to social pressures of "modernizing," of being technologically up-to date? More ashamed of our old antiquated ways? And yet, I want to cry, must we lose the charm, even the slightly primitive whiff that lives in the old bones? Is the new always better, and must we always *gut*, without any care for the kitchen's old story, let alone the tendons and ligaments that once connected it to the rest of the house? It's as if the kitchen is a patient, forever being opened up and tinkered with. How strange that the most unsettled site in a house might also be the one most rich with memories harbored deep in our own bodies. Where taste and smell are first engaged, those senses through which the past travels back to us. Proust's madeleine.

"Our son remodeled it for us," the Wilsons told us when we walked into the kitchen that first day, the day we fell in love with their house. Did we imagine a kind of helplessness in the tone of pride? As if to say, "We must bow down before the desires of the young, who will inherit the earth." I'm sure their son meant well, but in his zeal to make their later years more comfortable, he seems to have cut the kitchen off from the rest of the house, even from the dining room, which was so purely Craftsman that we discovered its identical twin in a book on the bungalow, right down to its glass-fronted cabinet and built-in sideboard, its pocket door opening into the living room, its long row of great wood-framed windows with a view to the north, of a welter of willowy blossoming trees.

But then we faced the great divide. To walk from the dining room into the kitchen was to turn a corner from a tender green bower into a too-well-lit world of work. The opening above the built-in sideboard that must have functioned, in old Professor Bouquet's time, as a pass-through to the kitchen, was now blocked off by a big piece of plywood, perhaps to keep the Wilsons' nine children at bay. I had a vision of Mrs. Wilson closing the dining room door, then sliding the piece of plywood across the pass-through and then saying to herself, *I am beyond their reach, just for a moment.* Oh, but whose notion of sanctuary was this? The ceiling was made of white sheet metal, with opaque fiberglass insets for fluorescent tube lighting. The floor was covered in Pergo, a laminate made to look like wood and withstand the weight of military tanks. Tall blond cabinets stretched to infinity, covering the place where, originally, there must have been glass-fronted cupboards to match those in the dining room. Yet despite its decor, the kitchen was still the room everybody clustered in whenever we had parties.

We found ourselves imagining how, if the glass-fronted cabinets were restored, the trembling evening light through the dogwood might refract off all that glass and pour into the dining room.

Then there was the matter of cooking together. The first time we tried, we found ourselves colliding around the butcher-block island anchored smack in the midst of the small kitchen, trying not to brandish our chopping knives. Craftsman kitchens are known for being small, utilitarian spaces, and this one was not sea enough to contain an island. Two people, no matter how recently and harmoniously linked, cannot cook together in a space like this without damaging each other. Our rhythms seemed to propel us toward the stove, the sink, and the trash can beneath at precisely the same moments, causing startling little collisions of hip and elbow. Tracy, a rock 'n' roll drummer, said, "It's not that I'm out of sync with you. Quite the opposite."

It was, I suppose, never meant to be a place for a couple to cook together. It was a housewife's sole domain of power, maybe even a refuge from the children.

I'm sure my mother shooed us out too, when she wanted to get serious about cooking. And we had a dining room, but it was reserved for formal occasions, or for the rolling out of dough for the annual adventure of kreplach soup, or "Jewish wonton soup," as it was known in our family.

But the kitchen was the true "warm spot" in the house, the place where we achieved, as a family, our slightly eccentric balance of solitude and community. My mother, for instance, created her own form of solitude within that communal space: she had designed the kitchen herself, so that she could cook on one side of an island, under a tall, sloped copper vent, and hand the food over the top of a diner counter like a line cook. My brothers and father sat on the other side: her customers. I myself, late-born and the last of four, had a little drop-down table in a corner nook, nestled between the refrigerator and the furnace closet, from which I could watch my mother (or vice versa), and see, albeit with some difficulty, the heads of the boys and men. This sounds idiosyncratic as I describe it now, but it suited us; we thrived on it. My mother prized deep quiet and salad: she preferred to eat her supper alone, late in the evening, listening to classical music on the radio. My father and brothers were hungry by 5 P.M., both for food and that form of conversation that sounds so much like argument to the uninitiated. I remember them ranged along the counter like football fans on a sofa, arguing some fine point or other as they ate. And what of myself, in the corner? It sounds like Cinderella's tale, I know, but the truth is, it was profoundly comforting. The side of the fridge was warm, and my mother put all my artwork up there with magnets. And behind me, the closet that held the furnace and brooms gave out a mysterious symphony of ticking, hums, and the occasional roar. I had all that I required at that young age: refuge and prospect, a window onto a world both familiar and strange.

Tracy's first memories are kitchen-rooted too, and, like mine, they perform a kind of intersection between the self and the family community. He remembers first the reddish-brown tile floor he was sitting on, at three and a half, when his grandmother handed him the telephone receiver and his mother's voice came on, to tell him he now had a baby sister. "I've changed my mind," he replied. "I want a baby brother instead." To console him, they brought him, along with the baby sister, a toy covered wagon to roll across the kitchen floor, over and over. And it was in that kitchen, a year or so later, that he got into his mother's Crisco and liberally smeared that baby sister with the stuff. "I greased her up good," he says, "and apparently she loved it; she just cracked up the whole time."

Needless to say, his mother was not so amused.

Who can say what combination of nostalgia, bruising, and oppressive lighting moved us to act? We had a little money saved, so, we thought, why not bring the kitchen back to the way it might have once been, at least in spirit? Let it glow as it once must have, full of natural light and *communicating*, as they say, with the rest of the house.

Thus it was that we found ourselves in the dining room with an interior designer recommended by Martha. He said many things, but the one that stuck with me was this:

"Can lighting is the opium of the masses."

We felt understood. As the days passed, he lent us beautiful books on early twentieth-century interior design. He soothed our economic terrors by reminding us that real Craftsman kitchens were "no big deal. Very simple, very utilitarian. Not big showcases." He won over Hannah with the promise of new tropical fish, when hers died. He became, briefly, a part of our family.

The day he handed over the sketches and put us in the hands of his favorite contractor, I felt bereft. It reminded me of saying good-bye to the midwife after Hannah was born. She had other cases, and gently, but firmly, cut me loose. So it was as the designer paused at our front door and said, "You can always call me, if you have other questions. Good luck."

We liked the contractor: this was Dave, an affable older gentleman in a back brace, clearly experienced and willing to put up with our innocence. He himself lived in a restored Craftsman bungalow, and exclaimed with pleasure over our dining room and living room. But we worried a little: he scratched his head over the designer's sketches, which, he said, were not really practical. We, of course, were no help at all; the practical had never been our forte. The metaphor of the midwife here wants to give way to that of the heart surgeon, rapidly outlining the double bypass, discounting the family doctor's wisdom along the way, like so much detritus. But eventually Dave made it clear to us that this was "perfectly normal": a designer's concept was always "something to play with," not writ in stone.

Soon after, Kid, the cabinetmaker, arrived on his Harley in a fringed leather jacket and ran his finger lightly, seductively along the various edges in the dining room. "Do you want them flat or coved," he asked. "In the dining room, they're coved."

"Coved," we cried as one. I knew our response had partly to do with the word itself: we both have a weakness for delicious words, regardless of their meaning. But this one sounds good for a reason. The little concave shape accepts shadows, heightens the glow on the wood around it. Coved, my God, I want the whole world coved.

He, too, frowned slightly over the designer's sketches. "Surely he didn't mean to leave you all this wasted space," he said. And he was blunt about the butcher block that would fit under the counter, to be rolled out as needed. "Ruins the aesthetics of the countertop," he said. "And gives us less cabinet space."

Still, leaving aside the fear, the endless attempt to gain knowledge through the asking of dumb questions, we felt the thrill of the quest; for the goal, in the case of this kitchen, was as much about recovery as it was renovation: a kind of home archaeology. We discovered, among other things, that half the kitchen had once been the original porch. The contractor uncovered, beneath the Wilsons' white-painted aluminum siding, the original narrow horizontal wood boards of the house, and we vowed that someday, someday, we would take off all the siding and restore that, too.

The first ten days of the renovation felt like nothing so much as a stint cooking in a campground. Very gently, Dave and his men removed our creature comforts, but just one at a time, so we'd get used to life without an oven and a fridge before he ripped out the stove and the sink. We put a big cooler full of ice on the back deck and borrowed a Coleman stove from friends. Up and out came the Pergo, and after that, three or four layers of linoleum. Off came the white metal ceiling and fluorescent lighting. French doors replaced the small window and door to the back porch. While the new appliances went in, Kid set about re-creating the glass-fronted cabinets, pursuing with great gusto the exact match of the wood stain in the dining room: that shining age-worn red-brown. He reminded me of John Berger's postman in the depth of his determination, his artistic obsession. It was hard, during that process, not to see the house as a body, having its passageways opened so light and air could come through.

It went on this way for some time, a delicate negotiation between the aesthetic impulse and the practical reality, a dance, I suppose, more crucial in kitchens than anywhere else. Slowly, we learned the art of compromise, of crafting a workable space with enough atmosphere to satisfy the spirit without substituting for it. Surely this could apply to other forms of union making.

One weekend near the end of the kitchen project, we came home from a brief getaway in Portland to find our deep green Vietnamese flowerpot, the one we'd bought on our honeymoon, busted, the little lemon tree lying on its side on the deck. "Hope this wasn't your favorite, sorry!" said Dave's note. Tracy and I mourned the thing briefly, and then shrugged it off. We looked at each other. Nobody needed to say it: if that's all that gets broken, we'll be lucky. And there was something else in it for me, a little saying I'd once heard: "The glass breaks so the person won't."

Already the kitchen felt more spacious, more like us and, most crucially, like the house. We'd told Dave that we wanted to paint the kitchen walls ourselves when the time came, and now, in preparation, we took a lesson in color-washing from a local housepainter. We went for the warmest combination we could find: "burnt sienna" for the undercoat, and a yellow charmingly called "warm toast" on top. Painting was a task for which we needed, once more, to be in sync. And we were, until nearly the end, when from sheer exhaustion, we bungled a part of the wall. The more we tried to fix the hideous spot, the more the paint came away, until we had a wound, a cancerous cell, on our wall, about eight inches across. I called our painting tutor in a panic. She said, "Sit down, breathe, and I'll tell you how to fix it."

I did as I was told.

"Ready?" she said.

"Tell us," I cried. "We're ready to do anything."

"Put a picture over it," she said.

In the end we arrived back at the question where it all began: the matter of light. This time not the light that would now pour in from the west at sundown, but the artificial light we'd need for nighttime, for deep winter dusks and mornings. Dave said, "Can lighting is cheapest and easiest to install—your best bet." But we were braced, not only by the designer's words to us but by Ann Cline's advice, delivered earlier that spring on our back porch. She'd shown us a catalog of Arts and Crafts–style fixtures from a Portland company, then made sketches for a simple lighting design: a triad of art-glass fixtures with a soft antique finish, one hanging down over the sink, one casting light upward in the center of the room, and a sconce to the side. A sweet, subtle symmetry, all with an amber glow. We held Ann's drawing and the catalog out to Dave. He sighed and agreed that the lights were beautiful, the design just right.

"But will you really have enough light to cook by?" he said.

"Yes," we said. "We'll make it work."

Whether or not the ghost of old Professor Bouquet, returning for a visit, would recognize his kitchen, we have surely taken it a step closer to its original anatomy. And there was one sweet, accidental surprise for me: Dave created a tiny alcove along one side, just around the corner from the cabinets, where I could fit my old writing desk, a small oak escritoire with secret cubbyholes and two inkpots. I remembered, with a jolt of pleasure, my childhood kitchen corner, so close to the warm, ticking furnace, where I ate, and did homework, and watched the family theater.

Refuge and prospect. The site of memory, and a place to make more.

Desire Lines

Late June. A letter arrives from a name half familiar. Peter Cline. I am too stunned to do anything but copy it out here, verbatim.

Dear Marjorie Sandor,

I write with very sad news. Ann died of a brain hemorrhage sometime Saturday morning, May 19. The coroner's autopsy offered only the consolation that it must have been quick.

Ann had so enjoyed the opportunity to deliver the lecture in Corvallis. I read many drafts, each better than the last. She told me of your hospitality, the beauty of Corvallis, and the pleasure of your company and that of your colleagues. A book on riverwalks, which she had read through on returning to Ohio and recommended, is now in San Diego with her good friend Wayne Rizzo. He flew out to help me with her large house.

Ann and I had met in nursery school at the YMCA in La Crosse, Wisconsin in 1946, dated occasionally in high school, reconnected in Seattle—1967—and married that year in London. Our marriage ended—1981—but not our friendship. Three days before she died, Ann, who had made a down payment on a retirement village condo in Oxford, came with me while I, too, signed a contract. We were to have adjoining units, to be finished in 2005.

Would you please share this sad news with others in Corvallis? I came upon your card, which Ann received just before her death, so I write you. Ann was a witty, sharp, imaginative, and kind person. She had a rich life, but it was too short.

Sadly,

Peter Cline

P.S. Miami U. is having a memorial service September 22. It plans to put her teahouse in the walled garden of the Music Library.

I feel stricken. Though I knew her only briefly, length of time doesn't seem to matter. I am fine for a while, then see her sitting on our deck, smoking her cigarettes, with that beatific expression, blessed by the pure play of ideas, and yet modestly amused by the whole business, as if a joke lies just out of hearing. I picture her, and a feeling of helplessness, of chaos, wells up in me, crests and breaks. In the waves, if I really dare to look, old losses bob up and tumble about. My father's death; my failure to fully love my first husband. All my fears about losing Tracy. About losing Hannah.

But there's something else in the waves; something to hang on to. Ann Cline was listening to something most of us cannot hear. I recall my architect friend's complaint after her talk, how, he'd said, "it didn't seem like she knew where she was going." I'm thinking now: *Well, maybe that's right, and was the great thing about it.* The painter Robert Rauschenberg once said that he felt "that art can be like furniture, static, clumsy. . . . For me, art shouldn't be a fixed idea that I have before I start making it. I want to include all that fragility and doubt that I go through the day with. . . . I want the insecurity of not knowing, like performers feel before a performance."

Maybe, from sentence to sentence, Ann was discovering where she was going, allowing the fragility, the insecurity of not-knowing, to be her companion. She couldn't help but follow an idiosyncratic path just slightly off the main one. *Desire lines*, another concept she taught me: these are the little trails people make in parks and gardens, off the prescribed paths that planners and landscape architects have so rationally laid out.

I will always be glad for the example of her particular form of disobedience. She lived with such heart and dignity, and gave pleasure and intellectual stimulation to so many. A cigarette, a piece of chocolate. A sigh of deep pleasure that moved all around a room of new friends. While she smoked her cigarettes on the deck, she looked with sly pleasure at the nimble, raucous blue jays. She listened in a way I will always hear now. Try to keep that memory close. How strange to think that if we had settled on the fall, instead of seizing the moment this May, we would not have met.

Gardener's Journal

July 2

A dream: I find myself in a green, steeply sloped, and symmetrical graveyard—a formal estate garden with gravestones is a better way to describe it. At the top of the graveyard, nestled into a hillside, is a little hut, and as I walk up to it, I see, in the window, a young man, eighteen or so, curly-headed and slender, with huge eyes. He glances up from some sort of work and seems startled, as if he recognizes me from somewhere. I come to the side door and he opens it. Mysteriously, he's trembling. I look behind him, where a lovely young African American woman is also at work, and I ask, "What are you making?"

"We make dolls," says the young man, still shaking. At last he touches my arm, and the shock travels all the way up to my neck. It's desire. "I just need a minute," he says and smiles, embarrassed. I touch his head, and say, "I have to go," and run off.

As I woke up, I thought, "What's it about?" Then I decided I didn't care. An angel making dolls in a pretty hut at the top of a graveyard. He knows you from long ago; he still desires you.

July 6

A week of neglect: of writing, of weeds. Hannah's in fine fettle, keeping busy with day camp and friends. And now it's nearly mid-

180

July. But the world seems a little unhinged, somehow, after Ann's death, and a few days ago, a friend of mine, the wonderful poet Aleida Rodríguez, told me on the phone that "Mercury is in retrograde," which means that travel is imperiled. I thought first off about how T was getting ready to travel to North Carolina for another teaching stint at Warren Wilson College. It is a marvel how a little phrase can inspire fear, superstition. We are not so modern as we think. I took T to the airport, all the time feeling this rising fear that something would happen.

At dawn the next day, the phone rang. It was Martha. She and her husband and their two young sons were driving home from the Portland airport at 3 AM when their car was struck by a huge semi. They are "all right," she said, as in alive and not too badly injured—and the kids, miraculously, were not hurt at all. But Martha has a badly bruised leg and Jon has three broken ribs and a separated shoulder. It's hard to say what psychological trauma they've endured, or how it will manifest itself as the summer goes on.

And there is the strangeness of taking care of injured folks in their own house, learning where the pots go, learning the rituals, what they need and live by. Going to get Martha and Jon at the hospital in this beautiful July weather brought back a memory not so much of T's surgery but of the rituals surrounding it: the ring road around the hospital, the entrance of the emergency room. It's a landscape so full of story for me that I felt a kind of familiarity, almost of habit. This must be common for people going through chronic illnesses: this sensation of getting to know the details and nuances of an institution—how close to feeling like "home" in some small weird essentials, even just those of any new habit—and how quickly we create habits, rituals, familiar patterns, to give ourselves whatever tiny notion of control we can.

July 15

I want to write about missing T. How different it is, down in the bones, my blood missing his skin, the weight of his arm. Primitive, like root thirst.

And in the midst of this fragile feeling, the garden has gone wild and intense with color, growth. The broccolis and lettuces are producing like crazy, we have green onions every day, and lemongrass and mint and thyme, even a first handful of cherry tomatoes. The headlong rush of it makes me want to hold still, take stock. It's been a full year since we moved into this house, a full year since T's heart surgery. Hold still and observe the garden, which looks and feels, well, like a real garden. The fence with the southern exposure is particularly wild: the dahlias are up and vigorous—dark red, salmon, pink, and lemon yellow—and next to the apricot-colored ones, the cherry tomato plants are behaving like climbers; they're four feet tall and it's only July.

Everything feels heightened: provisional and precious all at once, improvised and ceremonial. I make a trip to Garland Nursery with Martha. It's one of her first trips out since the car accident, and she's using a fine English thorn-stick cane, lent by a dear friend, to get around. Once there, we move slowly between the tables of perennials, admiring the mad profusion of high summer as if from a great, calm distance, buying nothing. She has great dignity with that cane: she looks like a marvelous writer of some other era, with her comfy loose black trousers and sweater, her cane, her chic short haircut. She is feeling better, putting weight on the foot, and calmly happy as we take a break, eat some popcorn on a bench by a little fountain, surrounded by plants. Afterward, when I bring her home, we sit for a few minutes on her garden bench. She lays down her cane, and for a moment, we don't speak at all; it is enough to sit here and look out at her garden, a grassy oval rimmed with daylilies, roses, tall spikes of angelica, plants whose names I don't yet know: an impression of wild intelligence.

But she's smiling, and in a moment she's on her feet, leaning on her cane and looking longingly at the stone path to her little upper garden, where she grows her vegetables in a little deer-proof enclosure. "Let's go up," she says. "Slowly, but let's go."

She has lettuces to give me, she says. She has way too much; her family can't eat it all. By the time I leave, I'm carrying a little handful of arugula seeds she saved from last fall and a big bag of spicy salad greens.

August 1

Dear God, please help me to stop buying new plants. Help me to become a pure waterer, weeder, and deadheader of our little plot, to mature from manic bride and bonnarder to the calm, the *jen*, of deep and ancient garden wifedom. Make it be enough to deadhead and to prop up the bee balm, which emphatically does not appreciate being watered from above. *Dayenu*, we say at the Seder table on Passover. It would have been enough had you brought us out of Egypt but not given us manna to eat. It would have been enough had you given us manna to eat but not delivered us out of the desert. Dayenu!

And it's true, I know it's true, that *to maintain* is now the task at hand. For it is August, and there is much drooping and bentness in the garden, among the dahlias, too, and even the sturdy lavender wands. I must apologize to everyone, lift up the fallen, and make a note to buy four tomato cages for next year, to get ahead of the completely lawless pear and Sun Gold tomatoes, not to mention the Spacemaster cukes, which were supposed to grow upright and bushy but snake along the ground insidiously. Yes, it is a purchase. But still a purchase in service of future maintenance, not of the new.

But then I see with horror that my lettuces are *stalks*, Eiffel Tower tall. The arugula has bolted, and this is my own fault—it was none other than myself who let it go, simply because the white blossoms looked so bright in front of the red carnations and the paprika yarrow. So on the list, beneath *tomato cages*, I find myself writing *new lettuces*. And no sooner does this phrase leave my pen than another follows: *green onions, cilantro, maybe some healthier basil for the window boxes*. And then because I am a human being, I rationalize my failure to resist. They (the basils in their boxes) have never been very happy this summer, as opposed to everybody in the beds. Then I write, as if guided by a devilish unseen hand, *one more fern* for the dry shade under the blue spruce. Then, since I'm going to Garland anyway, I figure I might as well take the opportunity to ask what vine, if any, could safely climb a blue spruce, and what, by the way, could rest between the two bloody-tissue plants as they grow, to shield our basement windows.

And when I arrive at Garland, what should I see first but a sign luring me to the tropical house, where hardy bananas are on sale? I am sorely tempted. What is wrong with me? A dark red tropical theme is emerging on one side of the Knight Gardener shrine, what with the cannas and all. And Martha's mammoth elephant ear near the blue spruce. And here in my hands are two little baby evergreen shrubs called Anisodontea Tara's Pink. I know now that I must plant the Jack Spratt flax somewhere else, and plant these two sweet shrubs between the Rose of Sharon bloody-tissue plants, to fill the gaps where a stranger could still peer into our basement windows.

One last thing, though, God help me, I should hold off till spring: I want to plant more Japanese anemones and bleeding hearts in the back garden. And here are more crocuses! By the time I'm done I will have planted about fifty. And they naturalize.

Color. I cannot get enough of it.

August 7

A few days ago, a young woman pushing an old woman in a wheelchair stopped by the front garden and plucked a flower, gave it to the old woman. I lingered on the other side of the street, voyeur of my own landscape in action—this is a particular pleasure. The act of gardening feels so interior, so meditative, that when you see it give a stranger pleasure, there's a little shock. The truth is, you never know to whom it will matter, or when, or, deepest of all, why. Must go move the sprinkler.

August 14

Kris called this afternoon. After nine months cancer-free, she's had another brain tumor show up, and the surgeon is going to "shoehorn" her into his schedule two weeks from now. She is matter-of-fact, even breezy on the telephone: the good news is that the tumor, like the last one, is very small and on the surface, this time between the lobes. "Apparently it's in yet another noneloquent part of the brain," she says, laughing. "Who knew there were so many?"

August 15

It's late at night. The dahlias are huge, haloed by the little security light on the back of Hillside house, as they were last summer. There is a small tree just in front of the light, and its branches move in the wind, giving the light an unstable, dappled quality. I look at everything wistfully. Any day now, they'll be demolishing Tento and Bryerly.

This is the elegiac light of the photographer Gregory Crewdson, in his night shots of suburbia. I seem to have become one of his characters, standing on my back deck looking helplessly at the dahlias, at the icy green light filtering through the little tree to touch them like some false sunlight in the dark.

Art sometimes trembles on the edge of madness. Think of synesthesia, the blurring of the senses, and Schumann's auditory hallucinations. The number 5 is purple, and midnight blue cries out *cigar*. Think of Bonnard, who once said, "Yellow is more than a color." And left it at that.

This is a summer meditation. Other forms of madness occur in darker seasons. In summer it is all confusion, a heady form of chaos, the abyss of too many voices, a dangerous abundance.

On Listening

The ear is the sense most active during periods of darkness, the last to cease functioning and the first to awake, capable of reacting to whispers even while a man is still asleep, the sense most closely linked with the emotional faculties, and with the forces controlling prudence, revenge, aggression, and also the appreciation of music.
—From the journal of Dr. Helbig, a Dresden homeopathic physician who treated the composer Robert Schumann's "nervous condition" in 1814

The ear is a neglected sense organ in our time. While we gaze at our computer screens and scan the newspapers for information, the ear works secretly, deep into the night, long after the rest of the body believes itself safely asleep. It is listening in the dark, the last of the senses to quit, and the one, apparently, quite eager to absorb the stories we don't even know we're telling. It hears and believes and doesn't stop there. If there is a dark gap, a growing lie or a secret pain, it goes right on ahead and scours a new channel for the future.

The composer Robert Schumann suffered from auditory hallucinations in the last terrible years of his life. Once he told his wife, Clara, that the spirits of Schubert and Mendelssohn were sending him new music from beyond the grave, but when she saw what he'd written out, she recognized it as his own composition from years before. In the long night of his last years, he was held hostage by something he himself made, but that he couldn't claim, couldn't even *hear* as his own.

By February 1854, he was plagued by tinnitus, a monstrous droning and roaring come to drag him under. But each night, just as he was falling asleep, the drone of that voice fashioned itself into the most sublime music, played by angels on unearthly instruments, like no human music ever heard; though when he got out of bed to write it down, it transformed into demonic trumpets, telling him he was a sinner, that they would cast him into hell. And then something worse: the demonic trumpets resolved into a final terrible note: A.

Not long after, he tried to drown himself, flinging his wedding ring, and then himself, into the icy waters of the Rhine. He was saved by two fishermen who happened by—though the story goes that he tried twice to fling himself out of their boat, and they had to physically restrain him. After his death a few years later, Clara found the note he'd written that night.

Dear Clara, I am going to throw my ring into the Rhine. Please do the same—then the two rings will be united.

What he wanted we can't know. But imagine the promise of silence after the demons and angels have had their way with you. The diminishment, at last, of their trumpets, and of the solitary, terrible A. Who hasn't felt it sometimes, the longing to go underwater, and stay there, offshore, in that muffled, pitch-black churning where we first began?

Gardener's Journal

September 6

Just an image of Kris.

Thursday, in Portland, she had her surgery. Saturday she and Rich came home from the hospital, and Sunday, T and I went over. Rich had built a lovely fire—the first of the fall—and I will forever see Kris sitting in her blue chair, in plaid flannel pajamas, between the fireplace and the big window looking out on Tenth Street. We helped ourselves to cups of tea in the kitchen, and came back to sit by the fire. A shy, soft-spoken man in glasses and a woolen vest was also there—a friend of theirs named Henry we've not met before. He and Kris were discussing Victorian fireplace inserts no one can afford, but how lovely. Rich went out, but came back shortly in his jacket and cap, carrying bags of groceries. He handed around more tea, and apple crisp another friend had brought.

Something settled over the room, took possession of it. For the moment, fear had been driven from it. You could feel the absence of the anxiety that clutches us most of the time. It fled in the face of this courage, and from the primitive requirements of healing. I remember this phenomenon from a year ago, the late summer and early fall of T's recovery from heart surgery: the way, for a little while, nothing but peace could enter the house. Something was at work to protect the wounded person. You felt it, you bent to it. What mattered—and what didn't—was briefly clear.

188

Kris and Rich's daughter arrived with her boyfriend. Another friend arrived. There were only arrivals, no departures, in that hour. But the image of Kris, just the image: as if in a dream I reach toward it, can't quite get there. I want to, and I don't. I want to stall this paragraph, leave it suspended, refuse the forward motion.

But here she is. Like a figure in one of her own paintings, in her flannel pajamas and slippers, in a soft blue chair, a red plaid blanket over her lap and knees. Blue eyes, fine high cheekbones, long hands. Sunlight coming from the high small south window above and left of the fireplace, sunlight touching her pale head, the stitches gummed at the edges with yellow hospital soap and blood and ointment. She wants to wash her head *now*, though the young orderly told her she should wait till tomorrow, but even this little consideration fades, can't bubble into tension against the settling of peace all around her, through her. On every table, books are stacked. I notice the big volume of M.F.K. Fisher, her aristocratic profile—this woman of appetite and endurance, in black and white. But there are other books, books I can't see the titles of, or I'd list them here. Other things, too: A box of comics about a superhero called Red Sonja, who has a bold stubby knife strapped to her thigh by a band of silver filigree. A cup of tea, a square glass baking pan of apple crisp. The fire finely, delicately crackling, like a sensitive accompanist. And behind Kris, framing her in the window, two sweet gum trees, one in her yard, another across the street: the sun lighting the leaves hot yellow, burnished red, the street still wet and shining dark and slate blue like one of our coastal rivers, yellow leaves drifting on its surface, bright from the morning's rain. The street Rich will look out at, in a few minutes, gesturing mysteriously with one arm. "The river must be perfect right now," he'll say, and we'll all reply *yes* to the water lit and glowing beyond the glass, beyond our vision, everything for the moment held in a Sabbath thrall.

September 12

Yesterday, yesterday, yesterday. We woke up to the radio this morning, the day after the hijacking of four jets, two flown into the World Trade Center towers and one into the Pentagon, also that mysterious crash in the Pennsylvania countryside . . . where was that plane bound? What further horror averted? Though it is hard to see it that way, horror enough. . . . On the radio this morning, Osama Bin Laden congratulated the people who did it but denied any responsibility.

Hannah, at the end of the evening yesterday, looked wide-eyed and exhausted as she went up to bed. She said she felt like her brain had gotten stretched. I thought we'd see her in the middle of the night, but we didn't. She slept through.

September 13

Hannah, last night at bedtime, even more exhausted than the night before, is more distressed by the words of our government leaders than by the images on the television. Their aggressive talk of war—protracted, difficult, the statements that countries who harbor the terrorists will be struck hard—all of this truly frightened her, and not because of what might happen here, exactly. "I don't want us to bomb people," she said.

She also said—and it took my breath away—that what happened here happens to other people in the world every day.

Rosh Hashanah, first day, 6 AM

The prayers last night looked different on the page. These sentences, which I used to recite with a kind of pure pleasure in the sounds of the words—"*Shelter us, O Lord, and thwart our enemies' plans, and make wickedness vanish like smoke*"—I now see were written by people who lived surrounded by fear, in a constant state of watchfulness with every expectation of being hurt, very soon. I hear the urgency, the actual prayer: please, God, don't let it happen to us again.

Out on the back porch. Though we were braced for it, the work on the Newman Commons, behind us, has been unnerving.

Although they saved the big elm and fir in the courtyard, several other trees have been bulldozed for the apartment building, cut down, taken away. And the two houses, Tento and Bryerly, were demolished on September 13. We walked over and watched Bryerly come down. At one point, the jaws of the steam shovel, having rammed several times into the side of the house till it collapsed, delicately lifted a computer monitor off an old desk left behind and set it neatly down on the pile of rubble. It was hard not to see, in that tiny moment, a distant miniature of the horror we struggle to imagine—all those office papers floating through the city and across to Brooklyn, landing in peoples' backyards, plastered up against the windows of a grade school.

October 1

Every morning, around three o'clock, I'm absolutely awake for an hour. The dream world is powerful; its images linger. In one, Hannah and I are lost in a tiny Oregon town called Nostradamus, and I am trying to call T on a wrecked old pay phone while a country hick in a high glass booth tries to distract me with crude remarks. A few nights later, another dream of being lost: Hannah and I are trying to go to the library downtown by bicycle. It is night, pitch-dark, and we have no headlights on our bikes. When we get there, the building has been torn down and where it used to be is a deep hole, lit by floodlights and traversed by narrow rickety planks, themselves splintered, to walk on. We see a professor from the English department; he has been wounded, his head wrapped in a bloody cloth. I wake up, and Hannah is standing by my bed, terrified by her own dream: a wild, white-haired person standing at the foot of the stairs, calling out, "Hello, Hannah"; then, in her own room, the desk overturned and a big black poodle on top of it. She's trying to call to us but can't make her voice come out, and then she thinks I'm coming up the stairs—she hears my ankles clicking (a trait I inherited from my father) and creepy voices in her room say, "She's coming," and disappear. She wakes up and realizes it was her clock ticking that sounded like my ankles.

It is hard to write, hard to reenter the private life, to claim it as a legitimate room. Today, in *The Dictionary of Angels*, I read about Nathaniel, the Angel of Fire. How prophetic the entry, how everything connects back to September 11. Is Nathaniel connected to Marc Chagall's *Descent of the Red Angel,* that painting in which an angel plunges from heaven onto an unsuspecting world?

What frightens me most is how I can't seem to grasp this moment, and all that it will change. How easily we slide back to our old American ways: on television, there are images of women executed in stadiums, the crowd roaring as a woman kneels in her pale blue veil. Then suddenly there's a commercial for a dental plan, a dog and a man playing tug-of-war with a rope between their teeth.

Hannah wakes up from a feverish afternoon nap and tells the following dream: she is in New York City, with a bunch of people—her dad and his new girlfriend and her two kids, and others, too—and they are walking in a park of some kind, only there are buildings, too, low ones, and the buildings are all made of glass and connected to one another, and inside plants are growing. They are office buildings, she says, but look like greenhouses. Most beautiful of all is a narrow alleyway made entirely of grass, long, deep green grass. It is totally silent in this place, she says, the most amazing silence; and then she says, "I knew where I was. It was the World Trade Center in the future, and in the silence I realized all those people—you know, Mom, all those people who died—were right there. They were all around us. It was sad, but peaceful too. I felt them there."

Epilogue:
The Late Interiors

[S]he is, in spite of herself, weighing the value of the word— the value of the gifts. Little by little she stows them tranquilly away. But there are so many of them that in time she is forced, as her treasure increases, to stand back a little from it, like a painter from his work. She stands back, and returns, and stands back again, pushing some scandalous detail into place, bringing into the light of day a memory drowned in shadow.

—Colette, *Break of Day*

*C*onsciousness, Bonnard scribbled in his daybook, *the shock of feeling and memory.* In his late still lifes and interiors, he chose to stay close to the objects of his studies, to dab at the canvas a little at a time, walk away and come back, so he wouldn't stray too far from the original impulse, that ephemeral thing always slipping away. It's been said of him that he didn't so much paint what he saw as paint what he remembered. So it is that gradually, over the long process of composition, his domestic scenes begin to shape an image, not of some recognizable place, but of the memories contained in their colors, their shapes. We see, at the edge of the frame, or feel the absence of, the wife who once poured tea from the teapot, or lifted the lid of the blue butter dish. So in the vibrant presence of the breakfast table, there is absence, too. The grief already dwelling in us,

193

and the grief we know is coming our way. For it will come. In what form we can't know. There is, finally, no way to prepare for it.

In his later years, after his wife's death, Bonnard turned more and more to the self-portrait, as if preparing the canvas for his own absence. Even when he paints his own shadowy self, bald and bespectacled and bare-chested, seated before the bathroom mirror, he is ever the withdrawn observer, the recording angel. As before, it's the little domestic objects on the shelf that hover and speak: the shaving brush, the bar of soap, the glass bottle gone faintly gold. These are the eloquent objects, heightened by the shadowy, naked human figure who watches them, quietly amazed.

What lies ahead? What treasuring up and what loss, and how will we endure it? How can we prolong the evening light flooding in through the dogwood?

The dogwood, which, to be honest, began to suffer blight in the ten years since I began my garden journal. Men come in a truck three times a year to spray it now. It is healthy again, but always desperately leaning away from the blue spruce, trying to get enough light. We trim back the spruce, but its vigor is astonishing.

Not long ago, Tracy bought me two copper cowbells to hang in our backyard. It took me a while to figure out where to put them. In the logical spot—a thick, low-hanging branch of the blue spruce—they were too well protected from the wind and rarely touched each other, and when they did, rang only faintly. One day I moved them onto a fragile, exposed branch of the delicate dogwood. And only then—vulnerable, unsheltered—did they make their music.

"To wait, to wait," wrote Colette, striving to learn how to fight the impulse to go after life, after love, to feed her sensual hungers as they arose. In her early fifties, the age I am now, she held her favorite fountain pen in her hand, the one with the softened gold nib, and did not write. Then she wrote, later, of not writing. In this way she learned, after a fashion, to wait, though this was not her natural inclination.

There are other forms of waiting to learn. We waited several years for a seed to germinate, take hold, in my womb. It didn't happen: like my mother in her late forties, I had two fibroids clinging to the uterine wall, blighting the growing place, and a hysterectomy was recommended. Still, in the midst of that disappointment, such joy at watching Hannah thrive and grow into a young woman.

We live with the doctor's words to Tracy after the heart surgery: his warning that the transplanted bypass vein eventually wears out, usually after ten years. *You'll let us know, won't you?* Not a day goes by that Tracy's chest muscles don't twitch or twang, a physical reminder of what he's been through, of what might lie ahead. Not a day goes by that I don't find myself registering the specific depth of his blue-green eyes, the color that blooms beneath his cheekbones. I remember how he once stood at our back kitchen window, holding out his arms, then bringing them in close to his body, as if to capture the last of the afternoon light.

Such thoughts propel me, on a midsummer day, out into the back garden, out to pull up the tenacious weeds starting up between the beds. The shepherd's purse and dandelions, the bunchgrass and oxalis. The ones whose names I've yet to learn.

These days, it's the act of prying away at the roots of the intransigent dandelions that calms me. Returns me to the present.

Listening helps too, and in this regard, the cowbells have been a great gift. They're the first music I can hear from this kneeling position: just behind me and over my head, they lightly knock into each other and produce a quiet lowing. Above them the dogwood rustles, and past that, the trees of the Newman Commons courtyard—the old elm and fir and that young aspen—rattle and whisper. The elm looks a bit fragile this year—fewer leaves, it seems to me. But the canopy is more or less intact, and sometimes there's singing in the new chapel back there, or the sound of an afternoon barbecue in front of the new apartment building. Hillside is intact, with all its mullioned windows, as are two other of Margaret Snell's cottages.

Painted pale green now, with white trim. Students live in one of them, and in the other are two seminarians and a priest, all from Argentina.

From farther out comes the slick swoosh of traffic on Monroe Street and campus, itself composed of many layers, the grinding of trucks bringing deliveries to Chemistry, the softer roar of cars, bicycles, skateboards, a blur of sandpaper and thunder. Voices human and animal, and at night, still, the pleasure cries of the young emerging from the pubs and cafés. We could swear they've gotten wilder in the past ten years. But it could just be that we're getting older. Soon we'll be white-haired professors with our earplugs firmly lodged.

I can't lift up my head to look; the weeds demand my full weight and attention. But I can see, in memory, the features of our little plot at this time of year, everything in full bloom: blue star creeper, night-blooming jasmine, purple clematis, a swath of Japanese anemone that expands each year, and must be lightly contained, but will last all the way into November. I can see the figures who populated this little place in its infancy, and populate it still: Martha, hands on hips, ever apologizing for the honeysuckle insurgency, for the vines have not only clothed the ugly chain-link fence but have scaled the Dearings' border shrubs, higher and thicker than either of us could have imagined. And Kris, who has used a mirror and great ingenuity to stamp an intricate mandala design on the bald spot left by chemotherapy, still comes over and asks anxiously, "Are you cutting down the clematis every year, all the way down, like I told you to?" I stretch out my arm, like a conductor preparing the orchestra, and invite her to observe the dark, healthy blooms, for the clematis, too, is crawling into the neighbors' trees, reaching for the sky. You could say, I suppose, that the garden has at last attained its maturity, and is beginning to enjoy a late-life beauty, the kind that can come only with age and use. It has attained that quality Ann Cline once described, in her book, as "a mutable and arbitrary beauty, begotten by use and familiarity."

Here, at last, is the wild and fully aged profusion I was so impatient for, ten years ago.

Bonnard loved to introduce one anomaly into the frame: The edge of a chair? The dark shape of the family dog? You can look at a painting of his for a long time. It can take hours, days, months before you are awake in the moment that the edge of chair reveals itself for what it plainly, poignantly is: the back of a woman's head as she walks away. A woman who also hovers in the other margin of the canvas, a teacup in her hand.

But the fact remains: it is the dark unidentifiable shape breaking the perfect symmetry of the composition that awakens memory's eye. Only then do you see what you missed before.

My cold hand reaching into garden soil. Beloved faces in firelight. A young girl in purple fleece and skates, her summer-brown legs in twilight. That same young girl, a little later, coloring bright autumn leaves on a black ground, discovering Eden beneath her own small hand.

Nineteen years old now, that child. A young woman headed back to college in the fall, in love with a dark-eyed boy. So it begins.

Vermilion in the orange shadows, on a cold, fine day.

How easy it is for us to miss things, as we walk the same road over and over. Only if we're lucky, only if for a moment we're not paying strict attention to our destination, does the foot catch on something and make us glance down, to see the strange-shaped stone. Once you see it, how can you resist the urge to pick it up, and put it in your pocket, and take it home to observe it at more leisure? To come back and find others like it and, on the spot, however you can, build a dream palace passing all imagination.

Once more, in memory, Hannah skims past me on purple skates, in a purple fleece. She is wild with life, racing away from me, toward a covered bridge. The path will take her close to the edge of a dark mass of trees. Someday it will carry her in. But not for many years, God willing, and not before she has given and received many gifts. Some will be recognized the moment they're given. Others, not till much later, the way it happens to us all, when we least expect it. Your foot catches on a stone in the path. Your hand, rummaging in a drawer for some document or other, alights instead on an old envelope, a letter saved from long ago, from a generous woman who once visited your town, your house. A woman who, before she left, took the time to show you where your new kitchen lights might go.

The feeling of shock and memory. A memory once drowned in shadow.

As I reread Ann's letter, I picture her sitting down at her own kitchen table to write it, her short, dark hair shining under lamplight. She doesn't know that this letter will be one of her last. Watch her with me a moment, as she takes up her favorite pen and sets it back down again. She weighs the value of a word. She treasures up her gifts.

Red tablecloth, brown teapot, blue butter dish. The light beyond her kitchen window shimmers, the same dark blue as the butter dish, suggesting evening or early morning. At last she takes up her pen again, the one with the softened gold nib. There's something more she wants to say to us.

Outside her kitchen window, the light deepens.

Night. Morning.

"Keep fixing the roof," she writes. "It shelters a magical story."

Acknowledgments

I owe an enormous debt to several generous, smart, patient people for their help along the way.

First, my great thanks to the visual artists Martha Lewis and Kristina Kennedy Daniels for their treasured friendship in and out of the garden, and to two beloved writer-pals, Suzanne Berne and Susan Jackson Rodgers, for their good counsel on long shop-talking hikes, rain-or-shine.

My thanks to Colleen Mohyde, a wise, kind literary agent who has stuck by me for a long time, and to Lilly Golden, the editor whose keen eye and ear have helped me tune not one book, but two. My thanks, also, to Bonnie Thompson, for the best copyediting imaginable, down to the last *Clematis jackmanii*. And my thanks to Nick Lyons, literary angel, for helping me find such a fine home for my work.

Back in Corvallis, the friendship of Ted Leeson and Elizabeth Campbell continues to be a delight and a refuge. To Ted I owe a particular thanks for his willingness to scratch his head over an early draft. He helped me see, through the murk, this book's future shape.

To my daughter Hannah I owe a debt beyond words. Her imagination and insight are, for me, the deepest source of light in this book.

Finally, my loving thanks to Tracy Daugherty, whose generous, brilliant tending of this garden of pages brought it to life.